OUR MASTERS' VOICES

Max Atkinson

OUR
The language and
MASTERS'
body language of politics
VOICES

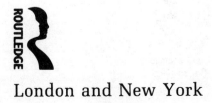

London and New York

First published in 1984 by
Methuen & Co. Ltd
Reprinted 1986

Reprinted 1988, 1989, 1991, 1994, 1996
by Routledge
11 New Fetter Lane,
London EC4P 4EE
29 West 35th Street, New York,
NY 10001

Typeset by Tradespools Ltd,
Frome, Somerset
and printed in England by
Clays Ltd, St Ives plc

*British Library Cataloguing in
Publication Data*
Atkinson, J. Maxwell (John
Maxwell)
  Our masters' voices: the
  language and body language of
  politics.
  1. Politicians. Public speaking
  I. Title
  808.5'1'088329

*Library of Congress Cataloguing in
Publication Data*
Atkinson, J. Maxwell (John
Maxwell)
Our masters' voices.
Includes bibliographical references
and index.
1. Political oratory.   I. Title
PN4193.P6A84
1984   808.5'1   84-6746

ISBN 0-415-01875-7

For Moira, Simon and Joe:
my favourite list of three

Contents

Illustrations

Foreword

This book is revolutionary. Those who have heard Max Atkinson expounding, with the aid of video tapes, his theses about the nature of stimulus and response for political speakers seeking applause, have their political lives transformed. They cannot go to a public meeting without listening for the antitheses and the triads that, when properly delivered, guarantee applause and, in the right circumstances, television coverage. Oratory is an ancient art. Demosthenes, Cicero and Quintillian offered instruction in the art of holding audiences and winning sympathetic reaction from them. But they did not have the advantage of modern technology to analyse systematically why particular styles or tricks worked. Oratory was a major academic subject for 2000 years. But over the last three centuries criticism has moved from the spoken to the written word. Now Max Atkinson has tried to redress the balance. He has added a new dimension to the appreciation of current politics. In an age when the public meeting, in the traditional Gladstonian form, is perhaps dying, he can show how forms of words, balance of sentences, rhythms of speech can induce an audience to applaud, almost irrespective of the intellectual content of what is being said.

But he has gone further. Public meetings may be withering away but people receive more communication about politics than ever before. Television and radio make the proceedings of government and parliament inescapable elements in the life of the watching citizens, glued to their sets for five hours a day. And politics on the box is dictated by what editors think the public will like. What better cue is there, as they select their material, than the phrases that won plaudits from a live audience? Max Atkinson has produced a guide that will influence both politicians and producers in shaping the material that we will all watch in the years to come.

His impact may be counterproductive or even immoral. Politicians may exploit his insights. Broadcasting people may be turned off by them. And we, the citizens, the recipients, may be made cynical by a raised consciousness of being manipulated. But the pursuit of knowledge cannot be abandoned because of the hazards of discovery. Academics must pursue truth wherever it leads without worrying about the unpredictable consequences of their findings. And, in this instance, when politicians are using their skills at communications to move, or even to deceive us, a heightening of our consciousness of their art is more likely to be beneficial than destructive. Cynicism is not an attractive quality – but realism may be. The democratic process demands popular skills in understanding the devices of persuasion. The more we can see through the tricks of charlatanry, the more likely it is that our politicians will have to take refuge in serious argument. There will be a steady escalation in the sophistication of audiences and the subtlety of orators. But it is more important to educate audiences (who tend to be unselfconscious) than orators (who do not). Max Atkinson has made a massive contribution to the process.

David Butler

Preface

We are nowadays more familiar with our political masters than at any time since government passed out of the hands of village elders. The mass penetration of television and radio has brought the sights and sounds of politicians directly into our living-rooms, and regular exposure to them has become part of the unavoidable background noise of contemporary life. Although George Orwell's nightmare world in which 'Big Brother is watching you' may have failed to materialize, the reverse is already with us: long before 1984, we had come to take it for granted that we live in a world where 'You are watching Big Brother' applies to all of us for at least some of the time.

Broadcasting technology has obviously transformed the nature of political communication by enabling politicians to air their views before a much larger audience than ever before. What is not yet so widely appreciated is that these same technological developments have also enabled us, their audience, to look more closely at the politicians themselves and at the ways in which they go about the business of trying to win our hearts and minds and votes. The aim of this book, therefore, is to show what can be learned about their communicative techniques by the simple strategy of watching and listening to them in a slightly different way than we have been accustomed to doing. As such, it is an exercise in political man-watching, and an invitation to others to do likewise.

With the aid of audio and video tape-recorders, the workings of various subtle processes can be brought more clearly into view, whereupon it becomes possible to begin to answer questions that previously seemed unanswerable. What kinds of political message are actually capable of striking chords with an audience? What are the most effective ways of expressing and delivering such messages? How do the skills of spellbinding speakers compare with those of their less charismatic competitors? Why are some passages from speeches singled out for quotation or replaying by the media – and why are some still remembered months or years later? What techniques make for an impressive television performance, and how do these compare with the more traditional techniques of platform oratory?

When I began studying political speeches, it never occurred to me that the results might shed some light on questions like these, let alone that I would end up writing a book about them. Originally, I began collecting tapes in a fairly haphazard way, for technical reasons associated with another research project on the workings of courtroom oratory and persuasive language. I had become increasingly intrigued by the question of how speakers in court manage, at least on occasions, to win the attention and approval of jurors. It is obvious enough that an ability to do this must play a critical part in the winning and losing of cases, but it is not so obvious how an observer can accurately distinguish between effective and ineffective speaking practices. The problem is that juries usually listen to the proceedings in complete silence, and therefore give little or nothing away in the form of audible responses to those passages in the talk that make an immediate and favourable impact on them. The student of courtroom language is thus deprived of any obvious clues as to what it is that strikes chords with jurors, and has to decide whether to proceed on the basis of his own intuitive impressions or to abandon such a line of enquiry altogether.

Reluctant to take either option, I hit upon the idea of looking at other kinds of public speaking where audiences are more vocal in responding positively or negatively to what a speaker says. Political speeches seemed to offer a promising starting-point because they tend to be punctuated quite frequently by clapping, cheering, booing and heckling. The fact that they are also regularly broadcast on television, especially during elections and party conference seasons, also meant that a large number of recordings could be made with relatively little effort.

Since then, a study which began as a small-scale by-product of another project has gone on to develop a life of its own. The sorts of observation reported in this book seemed surprising enough to be worth following up in a more systematic way, and this is now being done in conjunction with John Heritage and David Greatbatch of the University of Warwick. For some years, they have been using the same analytic techniques to study the workings of broadcast news interviews, and Heritage is now directing an Economic and Social Research Council funded project aimed at developing our earlier work on political communication. The data base has been expanded to include video recordings of the 450 or so speeches that were televised live from the three main British party conferences in 1981, as well as all the related news and current affairs programmes broadcast by the British Broadcasting Corporation and Independent Television during the same period. Some of the statistical results referred to in this book have been drawn from this larger-scale investigation, and I am very grateful to Heritage and Greatbatch for permission to publish a preview of these preliminary estimates.

As news of the study has spread, I have also had an increasing number of opportunities to give progress reports and show excerpts from the tapes to a range of audiences in various parts of Europe and North America. These lectures have regularly prompted three intriguing questions, none of which is dealt with at any length in the main part of the book. This does not mean that I think them unimportant, but is because we are not yet in a position to answer them with much confidence. However, as they are also likely to occur to readers, it may be useful to note what they are and what my own position on them currently is. The first question concerns the relationship between the findings reported here and the much longer tradition of analysing oratory and rhetoric that dates from classical Greek times, and whether this particular study amounts to anything more than the rediscovery of the wheel. The second asks whether or not my methods and results could be exploited by an unscrupulous Professor Higgins to perform a Pygmalion-style miracle and transform an ineffective political communicator into a successful demagogue. And the third involves the possible effects that knowledge about the techniques used by speakers might have on the willingness of audiences to produce favourable responses.

In response to the first of these, it can be noted that the present observations would have to be regarded as very suspect had they borne no resemblance whatsoever to earlier works on the subject. And although the main verbal techniques described here were known to the Greek and Roman rhetoricians, this does not necessarily mean that the whole of their wheel has been rediscovered, or even that we are on the way to an identical conclusion. In fact, a rather different picture is beginning to emerge, with oratory appearing to revolve around a wheel with a much smaller number of far more powerful spokes than the one depicted in the classical texts. By this I mean that a more exclusive concentration on passages from speeches which actually prompt an immediate audience response shows that there are far fewer effective devices than had previously been thought.

This difference almost certainly arises from the fact that recording technology has only recently become available to students of oratory. This has made it possible to carry out much more detailed studies of actual *oral performances*, whereas there was formerly little choice but to rely heavily on *written texts* of famous speeches. However carefully one examines a text, there is no way of identifying which passages and which particular verbal formats struck chords with the audience while the speech was being delivered. As a result, those who have had to work without the benefit of recordings have tended to adopt an encyclopedic approach to the description and classification of rhetorical devices, and their studies typically list many scores of types and sub-types. But exactly how many and which ones of these regularly work to elicit an immediate audience response is not yet known for certain. One of the preliminary results from the present study is that three out of every four displays of approval occur in response to about half a dozen verbal devices, and that those described in this book prompt about half of all bursts of applause during political speeches. For a fuller and more accurate estimate, however, we shall have to await the results from the follow-up study mentioned above.

The question of how far this study could be exploited in training politicians to become more effective speakers is also one to which no definite answer can be given at present: as far as I know, it has not yet been tried. However, it would seem that the findings already have some fairly clear implications that could be capitalized on by speech-writers. They also suggest that it is perfectly possible to carry out 'diagnostic' analyses of an individual's strengths and weaknesses, which could presumably be used in the design of tailor-made coaching programmes aimed at improving his or her performing abilities.

Such a possibility has led some people to point out that there are serious ethical dangers in pursuing this kind of research at all. However, if there are powerful regularities in the workings of political communication, it would seem to be advisable to find out as much as we can about them – and to do so *before* they are discovered by people with a vested interest in keeping quiet about them in order to use them in the service of their own political ambitions. Publication of this book may therefore involve some risk that aspiring politicians will be able to pick up useful tips about speech-writing and delivery. But I tend to think that this is outweighed by the importance of informing audiences about the communicative techniques to which they are exposed, and to which we all appear to be remarkably vulnerable.

This brings us to the third question of whether audiences who are better informed about the workings of rhetorical devices would react any differently when they notice a speaker using them. Would they, for example, be inclined to pause for longer in order to give more serious consideration to whether it was the contents of a message or the manner of its delivery that made it appear to be worth applauding? The answer to this is something that I hope individual readers of this book will be able to find out for themselves. And if my observations do make them pay closer attention to politicians in the future, the study will have been well worth doing.

A project of this sort obviously depends on the inspiration and support of many other people, and the present investigation has only been made possible by the development of a new approach to research that has become known as 'conversation analysis'. A guide to further reading in the area, as well as to what is involved in pursuing such work, is provided in appendices II and III. Meanwhile, I would like to express my gratitude to colleagues on whose research I have drawn and whose encouragement has contributed towards the completion of this particular project. In alphabetical order, they include Judy Davidson, Paul Drew, Charles Goodwin, Marjorie Goodwin, David Greatbatch, Christian Heath, John Heritage, Gail Jefferson, William O'Barr, Anita Pomerantz, Emanuel Schegloff and Rod Watson. Others whose comments, support or advice have been greatly appreciated at various stages in the preparation of the manuscript are Robert Baldwin, Ben Beaumont, Anthony Bladon, John Boal, David Butler, Ivor Crewe, Robert Dingwall, Donald Harris, Margaret Harvey, Caroline Henton, Eric Kendrick, Tony King, Christine Lee, David Lee, Paul McKee, Desmond Morris, P. J. Shaw and William Twining. I am also grateful to Noël Blatchford for remaining cheerful while typing what I hope will be the last thing I ever write without the aid of word-processing technology.

Although the work has been done mainly on a part-time basis, the Economic and Social Research Council, through its funding of the Centre for Socio-Legal Studies, has played a crucial facilitating role by providing an environment within which it has been possible to develop these interests.

My biggest debt is, as ever, to my wife and children for having suffered my obsessions with such patience and good humour for so many years.

Max Atkinson
Oxford, 29 February 1984

Postscript, 1986

It is no longer the case, as it was in 1984, that no one has tried out the practical implications of this study.

The most public test to date was featured in a Granada Television documentary produced by Gus Macdonald, with whom I collaborated in using the book as the basis for a course of training for a novice with no previous experience of public speaking. Key parts of the process leading up to Ann Brennan's speech at the 1984 conference of the Social Democratic Party were then filmed for the *World in Action* current affairs series and screened on 24 September 1984. Mrs Brennan was applauded so much that she had only got two-thirds of the way through her speech when the chair intervened to say she had run out of time – at which point she became the only non-platform speaker to win a standing ovation at that year's SDP conference.

On its own, of course, the outcome of a single experiment cannot be claimed as definitive proof that this kind of research has significant applied implications. However, letters from readers and other responses since the book was first published suggest that there are quite a number of people who have found its contents of direct practical use to them. The main findings have also stood up remarkably well in the face of the searching statistical investigation by John Heritage and David Greatbatch (see their 'Generating applause: a study of rhetoric and response at party political conferences', *American Journal of Sociology*, Summer 1986).

Taken together, these various developments provide grounds for optimism about the growth of public and scientific interest in the methods and findings of conversation analysis, both pure and applied.

Acknowledgements

The author and publisher would like to thank the following for their kind permission to reproduce copyright material:

Associated Press Photos for plates 4.4 (the Martin Luther King photograph only) and 6.5; the British Broadcasting Corporation for plates 3.1, 3.2, 3.4, 3.5 and 4.3; the *Guardian* for plates 5.2 and 5.3; Independent Television News for plates 1.3, 2.2, 4.1, 4.2, 4.5, 6.2, 6.6 and 6.7; Mirror Group Newspapers for plates 5.1 (the *Daily Mirror* facsimile only) and 5.4; Novosti Press Agency for plate 1.2 (the Lenin photograph only); Popperfoto for plates 1.1, 1.2 (the Mussolini, Castro and Hitler photographs only), 1.4, 2.1, 2.3, 3.3, 4.4 (the John F. Kennedy photograph only), 6.1, 6.3 and 6.4; the *Sun* newspaper for plate 5.1 (the *Sun* facsimile only).

1 Politicians in need of attention

Observing political speakers

An ability to speak effectively in public is one of the oldest and most powerful weapons in the armoury of professional politicians. Leaders of nations, political parties and mass movements have traditionally been those who emerged as the most convincing spokesmen for their cause. Obvious examples from the present century include Lenin, Hitler, Mussolini, Churchill, de Gaulle, Castro, John F. Kennedy and Martin Luther King. As politicians they represented a very wide range of opinions and beliefs. But one thing they all had in common was a quite extraordinary ability to captivate their audiences, inspire crowds and mobilize mass opinion.

Few people ever master even a few of the technical skills necessary for composing and delivering a spellbinding speech. Yet the vast majority of us have no difficulty at all in recognizing an effective public speaker when we see one, even

1

1.1 Political leaders have traditionally been those who proved themselves to be the most effective spokesmen for their cause.

Winston Churchill

Martin Luther King

Charles de Gaulle

John F. Kennedy

1.2 Skilful public speaking can be readily recognized even in those whose politics we may disagree with, and whose languages we do not understand.

V. I. Lenin

Fidel Castro

Benito Mussolini

Adolf Hitler

though we may thoroughly disagree with the political views of the particular person in question: we do not have to be Nazis or Fascists, or even fluent in German or Italian, to be able to see from the old newsreels that Hitler and Mussolini were very talented orators. We can also be fairly confident that we will not be alone in our judgements, and that others will come to similar conclusions about which speakers are inspiring and which ones are boring. Indeed, if large numbers of people did not react to public speaking in a more or less identical way, it is quite impossible to see how anyone would ever succeed in establishing a reputation as a brilliant orator.

The fact that we are able to appreciate effective public speaking means that we must have some kind of technical awareness of the methods underlying the production of an electrifying or tedious performance. But exactly what these methods are is a question that most people probably never bother to ask themselves: they can see perfectly well that some speakers inspire their audiences while others do not, and that is all there is to it.

The aim of this book, however, is to show that this is certainly not all there is to it, and that assessments of the relative merits of different political orators derive directly from their use of particular verbal and non-verbal techniques – techniques that we readily recognize and respond to as members of an audience listening to a speech, but which we are none the less hardly aware of at the time. Many people will no doubt already have a vague and uneasy suspicion that something like this must be going on, and that this is why mass audiences are so vulnerable to the rhetoric of demagogues. The starting-point of this study, then, is the view that the way politicians communicate with the public has been shrouded in too much mystery for far too long, and that modern recording technology has provided the necessary instruments to start peeling the shroud away.

The advantage of audio and video tape-recorders is that they enable us to subject what politicians say (and how they say it) to much more detailed scrutiny than has ever before been possible. They also permit access to the *interaction* between speakers and audience, by making it possible to examine displays of approval (such as laughing, cheering and clapping) and disapproval (such as booing, jeering and heckling) with a view to finding out exactly how such responses were prompted by the way a politician was speaking. All this might sound like the most tedious and pointless enterprise imaginable, suitable only for a hardened and most peculiar type of masochist. But it must be remembered that similar observational studies of animal behaviour have enabled zoologists to make many remarkable discoveries about regularities in the animal world. These include a good many findings about the patterns of dominance among different species of animals, from the pecking orders of farmyard chickens to life-and-death struggles between potential pack leaders in the jungle. Given that so much can be learned about animal politics by observing animals in their natural habitats, it is reasonable to expect that a great deal may also be learned by adopting a similar approach to the study of human politics.

In some respects, of course, this is easier said than done: the natural habitats of human politicians are obviously much more varied than those inhabited by their animal counterparts, and some are so private that an outside observer would never be allowed anywhere near. Fortunately, however, a great deal of the behaviour of politicians takes place in public, which means that we do not have to await permission to eavesdrop inside Downing Street or the White House before work can begin. Nor do we have to embark on expensive or uncomfortable expeditions in order to make our observations. Thanks to the broadcasting media, anyone with a radio or television set is already in a position to collect specimens of the public performances of politicians in the comfort of his own home. And, with an audio or video tape-recorder, a large collection can be quickly accumulated and preserved for closer inspection.

Once a speech has been recorded, it can be studied with all the advantages that television viewers of an action replay of a sporting incident have over those who were actually present at the event. The players and spectators only see it fleetingly, as it is happening, but television viewers get a chance to look at it again and again. Finer points that may have been missed the first time around are brought into sharper focus as the action is replayed, slowed down, or frozen for even closer inspection. While footballers and spectators may know who scored a goal, they often have no more than a vague impression of the events leading up to it. By contrast, viewers of the action replay can track the sequence as it unfolds and see exactly how the different actions were organized and combined to produce the goal. They are thus able to achieve a degree of understanding of how a particular move worked that is simply not available to those who saw it only once.

All this applies equally to the study of any other form of human behaviour that can be preserved on video tape, including the behaviour of politicians. If, for example, the saying of something which results in applause is to the political orator what scoring a goal is to a footballer, then action replays can be put to work in a similar way by looking to see how the words, gestures and other bodily movements were combined together to produce the desired response.

Another well-known feature of the action replay is also crucially important for the way the observations reported in this book should be read and evaluated. Replays of sporting incidents are almost always accompanied by a further commentary on the events we are seeing again, the object of the exercise being to supply a more detailed and informed analysis. But viewers can also see the sequence of events for themselves, and are therefore in a position to draw their own conclusions about what actually happened, as well as to judge the adequacy or otherwise of the commentator's description and analysis. If his claims about how the event occurred are out of line with what the viewers saw, the television company's switchboards are likely to be jammed within a matter of minutes. And, if a commentator persists in making excessively personal, subjective or eccentric observations, he is unlikely to hold down his job for very long.

The capacity to replay a sequence of action therefore serves as a powerful constraint on what an observer can get away with saying about it. The fact that any particular observation can be directly and immediately checked upon by anyone else who sees the replay means that the analyst's descriptions have to fit in with what everyone else can see for themselves; otherwise his claims may be exposed, criticized or ridiculed for being hopelessly inconsistent with the evidence on tape. In a book like this, of course, it is impossible to supply readers with copies of the original recordings on which the study is based, and the best that can be done is to illustrate the main points with reference to pictures and verbatim transcriptions. It is therefore important to emphasize from the outset that these are included not just for illustrative purposes, but also to give readers an opportunity to check on the adequacy or otherwise of my descriptions of them – in much the same way as they might evaluate what a sports commentator says about the events featured in an action replay. Exceptionally sceptical or curious readers may also be moved to scrutinize the findings more closely by compiling their own collection of recordings.

Keeping audiences awake

Our capacity to appreciate televised action replays of a goal being scored obviously depends to a great extent on our knowing something about the basics of the game of football. So too, as we look at replays of politicians making speeches, do we need to have an understanding of what is basic to the particular game being played. At the very least, we must have some idea about what they are trying to achieve, and the obstacles they have to overcome in order to succeed.

At first sight, the answer to such a question may seem to be too obvious to be worthy of serious consideration: the professional politician is clearly out to win power, and this can only be done by persuading more of the people that more of his policies have more to commend them than the rival packages of his opponents. But this ignores the fact that none of these things is possible unless regular victories of a much more basic kind are achieved in situations where audience attentiveness is at stake. For the speaker who proves himself to be incapable of holding the attention of live audiences stands little chance of winning their approval. And without the approval of others the most essential part of a politician's life-support system is missing.

This suggestion that there may be something absolutely basic about holding the attention of an audience is supported by the fact that it is something that has to be done not just by political orators, but by *all* successful public speakers. This is because public speaking has an immense potential for boring audiences, as is well known to anyone who has ever fallen asleep during a

1.3 Successful politicians must be able to hold the attention of as many as possible of those in the audience, but even prime ministers like Margaret Thatcher and James Callaghan are not always 100 per cent successful.

speech, sermon or lecture. The problem arises from the fact that such talk goes on for an extremely long time compared with the modes of speaking used in the course of most human communication. The types of verbal exchange with which we are all far more familiar involve much shorter bursts of talk, and only comparatively rarely is it difficult to remain attentive to what someone is saying during a conversation. However, one situation where attentiveness regularly can become a problem, even during everyday verbal exchanges, is where a person talks *too much*: talking too frequently or for too long tends to be regarded as a highly undesirable characteristic, and provides the basis for complaints that a person 'hogs conversations' or is 'long-winded', 'rambling' or 'boring'. This supports the view that there is a general preference for brevity and succinctness in human communication. Speeches and related forms of talk can therefore be seen to represent, almost by definition, a potentially unreasonable imposition on the tolerance of listeners – at least until or unless the speaker is able, through his performance, to prove otherwise.

Crucial to understanding the potential for audience boredom in the face of one speaker speaking for an extended period of time is the realization that such situations involve a general weakening of the basic incentives to pay attention that work perfectly well for most other types of verbal interaction. In conversations, for example, anyone who is not currently speaking may either wish, or be called upon, to speak next. This means that it is necessary for a person to know not just exactly *when* it would be appropriate to start speaking, but also *what* would be a suitable thing to say when the moment comes. Failure on either of these counts is likely to have serious consequences for an individual's reputation, as others can use it as evidence that he or she is not paying attention, and is therefore 'impolite', 'bored' or even 'socially incompetent'. So long as people wish to avoid attracting such accusations, they have a powerful incentive to pay attention whenever they might get the next turn to speak.

By contrast, in settings where there is little or no chance of getting a turn to speak at all, let alone next, there is much less incentive to pay close attention to what is being said. Many of the techniques deployed by effective public speakers thus appear to be designed to attract, sustain or upgrade the attentiveness of audience members who might otherwise be inclined to go to sleep. At the same time, collective activities like clapping and booing can be used as a substitute mode of response by people who are deprived of any individual opportunities to speak. Such displays of approval and disapproval therefore also provide audiences with an in-built incentive to pay attention very similar to that imposed by the possibility of

11

having to speak next during an ordinary conversation. As will be seen later, audience responses do not occur randomly, but are found at specific points in the course of a speech, and the degree of precision timing involved can only be achieved by paying very close attention to the preceding flow of talk. The public outrage about the rowdy behaviour of British members of parliament that has followed the broadcasting of debates has thus failed to take into account the way in which such noisy traditions may work as an extremely efficient incentive for politicians to pay close attention to the proceedings, even when they may have little or no chance of being officially called upon to speak next.

As this book is primarily concerned with the way political speakers and their audiences behave at large-scale party rallies, it is important to bear in mind that the problem of holding attention is directly related to the number of people involved: in general, the bigger the audience, the more difficult will it be for speakers to secure and sustain the attentiveness of everyone there. As the size of a gathering increases, the audibility and visibility of the speaker, both of which are important if audiences are to be able to follow what he says, become progressively more of a problem. Architectural design features (like raised platforms for speakers and banked rows of seats for the audience) and audio-visual aids (like amplification systems and slide projectors) can only go so far in resolving such difficulties. They are of little use if a speaker fails to gear his performance towards assisting the audience to remain attentive. To do this successfully a speaker must, among other things, be able to keep as many of the audience as possible under constant surveillance. Because people may find it embarrassing to be caught out going to sleep or reading a newspaper, scanning the audience is one of the ways a speaker can increase the pressure on them at least to look as though they are paying attention. It also has the considerable advantage of revealing signs of boredom, puzzlement or disbelief, to which speakers can instantly respond with a suitable joke, explanation or elabora-tion. At very large rallies, where the speaker may be unable to see many of the audience, who in turn cannot see him either, it is even more difficult to make such strategies work effectively: fewer signs of audience inattention and dissatisfaction will come to the notice of the speaker, while people will simultaneously feel freer to go to sleep without fear of public exposure.

From the point of view of describing how effective political oratory works, there is therefore much to be said for concentrating on passages from speeches where audiences laugh, cheer or applaud. For the occurrence of such responses provides concrete evidence both that they had been paying attention to the immediately preceding talk, and that it made a favourable impact on them.

A barometer of attention and approval

For politicians, responses like clapping and booing provide an important barometer of their popular appeal. Depending on whether they are greeted by frequent bursts of applause, heckling or complete silence, they will be deemed to have had a rapturous, hostile or indifferent reception. The development of an individual's political career may therefore be profoundly influenced by which of these assessments is arrived at by party managers, media reporters and the public at large.

Politicians themselves are, of course, well aware of the critical importance of audience reactions, so much so that some of the more unscrupulous ones have been known to go to considerable lengths in manipulating them for their own ends. In the early days of Nazism, for example, Hitler used to be as provocative as possible at the beginning of his speeches, so that any opponents attending his rallies could be identified and flushed out. Those daring to show their disapproval by booing or heckling were promptly jumped on and removed by henchmen who had been specially detailed to perform such duties. By the time Hitler reached the climax of his speeches, the chances of dissent had thus been eliminated, leaving the way open for nothing but favourable responses. In later years, applause manipulation facilities were actually built into the design of the Nuremberg stadium. Strategically positioned microphones were wired to amplifiers hidden behind the rostrum, so that technicians could beam the cheers and chants of 'Heil Hitler' back at the crowd through loudspeakers. This not only had the obvious effect of increasing the volume of the favourable responses, but it also made the assembled multitude

13

1.4 An ability to inspire audiences is less important for politicians who can stay in power without subjecting themselves to free elections (clockwise from top left: Leonid Brezhnev, Yuri Andropov, Konstantin Chernenko).

clap and cheer louder and longer than they would have done without any such additional prompting. This obviously had great advantages from the point of view of the Nazi propaganda machine because the artificial source of the increased fervour remained invisible to the newsreel cameras, which meant that the millions who were subsequently exposed to films of the rallies were completely unaware of it.

The fact that an orator as successful as Hitler took audience responses seriously enough to devise ways of manipulating them does not necessarily mean that such practices are in widespread use. It does, however, underline the basic importance of such reactions in the development of a politician's image and career as a popular figure. It should also alert us to the relative ease with which displays of approval can be interfered with and manipulated to enhance a speaker's reputation.

The following chapter concentrates on regularities in the behaviour of audiences, and on how applause is responsive to a

very narrow range of political messages. The focus then shifts in chapter 3 to the most effective verbal and non-verbal methods for packaging and delivering such messages. Subsequent chapters deal with how the use of these techniques features in the speaking styles of 'charismatic' leaders (chapter 4) and in the selection of passages for quotation in the media and elsewhere (chapter 5). The final chapter then suggests that the techniques which make for effective live oratory are not necessarily compatible with coming across effectively on television, and that we are therefore witnessing a major change in the basis on which political leaders are selected. For the most part, totalitarian political systems which have survived beyond the first generation of revolutionary leaders are excluded from consideration. This is because the ability to inspire audiences and win public approval becomes less important once politicians are in a position to sustain themselves in power without subjecting themselves to free elections.

2   Appreciation in the usual manner

Responding in unison

In the early 1960s, the comedian Spike Milligan starred in a West End play called *The Bed-Sitting Room*. At the end of each performance the curtain stayed up, and there was a great deal of confusion among the audience as to whether or not they should start clapping. The general uncertainty was intensified when Milligan came to the edge of the stage and began to play 'God save the Queen' on a tin whistle. The problem now confronting the audience was whether or not to stand up and show the customary respect for such a bizarre rendition of the national anthem. Coming at the end of the play, there was no doubt that it was occurring at the right time in the proceedings. But the instrument and the performer seemed too comical for the performance to be treated in the usual manner. The result was a period of chaos during which some people stood up, some remained seated and some hovered nervously in between. And whichever option was chosen, it was impossible for anyone not to feel highly conspicuous, and at least some degree of embarrassment.

This cleverly stage-managed incident provides a dramatic illustration of the fact that we tend to feel very uncomfortable when, as members of a collectivity, we fail to co-ordinate our own behaviour with that of everyone else. It is the sort of experience that will be familiar to anyone who has ever stood up just at the point in a church service when the rest of the congregation knelt down, or who has started clapping at a concert after the fourth movement of what subsequently turned out to be a five-movement symphony. When we are seen to step out of line, we draw attention to our ignorance of how to behave properly on such occasions, and may find our social competence called into question. It threatens us with exposure to the horrors of public ridicule and humiliation before those who did know what to do next and when to do it. At public gatherings, there is thus considerable pressure on all those present to conform and 'go along with the crowd'.

The failure of the curtain to come down at the end of *The Bed-Sitting Room*, coupled with the performance of the national anthem by a comedian playing a tin whistle, effectively demonstrated how easily a sequence of events can be disrupted by relatively minor modifications to procedures which usually enable a large group of people to do the same thing at the same time. Certainty about what to do next and when to do it was replaced by ambiguity, and members of the audience were forced to endure the kind of embarrassment associated with being seen to break ranks – an experience which in this case became only slightly more bearable with the realization that it was equally impossible for anyone else to do otherwise.

The strong pressures on members of an audience to act in unison, and the fact that it takes very little to interfere with their capacity to do so, have important practical consequences for the sorts of things that can actually be done at public meetings. In particular, people are largely restricted to doing only those things that can be easily co-ordinated in such a way as to be *done together*. To this end, special aids are often used to make it easier for large groups of individuals to act as one. It is, for example, no coincidence that music features prominently

2.1 Individuals in an audience are under immense pressure to act in unison as in the case of this crowd saluting Hitler at a Nazi rally in the 1930s.

across a very wide range of public gatherings, from military parades and church services to street carnivals and football matches. A recognizable rhythmic beat, sometimes in combination with the familiar words of a hymn or popular song, makes it possible for thousands of different individuals to join in and produce exactly the same actions at exactly the same time.

As we begin to look in more detail at audience responses, it becomes evident that the most usual ways of showing collective approval and disapproval are also characterized by common features which enable them to be produced by a large number of people at the same time. Cheers and boos, for example, are made up of very extended vowel sounds, as in 'Hooraaaaaaaaaaay!' and 'Booooooooooooo!' Their open-ended character therefore makes it very easy for people to join in some time after a roar has

2.2   Like booing and jeering, applause is an essentially
collective activity: one person can clap hands, but it only
becomes applause when others join in.

got under way. By so doing, even late starters are able to play an active part in determining the volume, intensity and duration of a response. Similarly, applause is an essentially collective form of behaviour: one person can clap his hands, but it only becomes applause when several do so repeatedly and at the same time.

Collective displays of appreciation

When someone concludes a vote of thanks by saying 'Let us now show our appreciation in the usual manner', the audience knows immediately that the time has come to start clapping. This particular way of issuing such invitations may have become an over-worked cliché, but it contains within it an important truth about the nature of applause: of the various methods available to us for showing our collective appreciation and approval, applause is indeed the most usual one. This is reflected both in the regularity with which it is used, and in its capacity to drown out and take over from any other responses that may have started up at about the same time. In fact, when we look more closely at how applause gets under way, it emerges that a main function of other affiliative responses is to prompt audiences to start clapping. Even when no official cheer-leaders have been appointed, individuals who whistle, laugh, cheer or shout 'Hear hear', effectively perform the same task of leading the rest of the audience into a collective response.

These points can be illustrated by looking at some actual examples, which also provide a preliminary opportunity for readers to familiarize themselves with the main symbols used for transcribing the extracts included in this and subsequent chapters. Before turning to the first example, then, it should be noted that applause is represented by a string of crosses, small and large ones being used to indicate soft and loud clapping respectively (xxXXXXxx). A dash on either side of a cross (-x-) represents an isolated clap, and several in a row refer to a period of hesitant or spasmodic clapping (-x-x-x-). Square brackets linking two lines show the exact point at which a new activity starts in relation to the previous one. In extract (1), for example, the position of the bracket indicates that the applause for Neil

Kinnock, who had just been elected leader of the Labour Party, started just after a second beat of laughter. The applause then took over completely, and lasted for a further seven seconds (indicated by the line and number in brackets above the applause):

---

(1) (Labour Party conference, 1983)

Kinnock: Doctors ... are injecting monkey cells into the ageing rich in order to rejuvenate them, a very complex process. It's obviously failing with the Tory cabinet.

Audience: Hah hah ⌈hah hah ⊢————————(7.0)————————⊣
Audience: ⌊xxXXXXXXXXXXXXXXXXXXXXXxxxx-x

In the second example, the same symbols show that an eight-second burst of applause for Margaret Thatcher is triggered by and starts in the middle of a cry of 'Hear hear':

---

(2) (UK general election, 1983)

Thatcher: There's no government anywhere that is tackling the problem with more vigour, imagination and determination than this Conservative government.

Audience: Hear ⌈hear ⊢————————(8.0)————————⊣
Audience: ⌊xxXXXXXXXXXXXXXXXXXXXXXXXXxxx-x

The first bracket in extract (3) indicates that the initial response starts even before the speaker has finished, and the second pair of brackets shows the point at which the applause bites into both the talk and the shout of 'Hooray' (capital letters indicate louder speech):

---

(3) (British Academy of Film and Television Arts award ceremony, 1980)

Announcer: ...SHIRLEY RUSSE⌈LL FO⌊R YANKS
Audience: ⌊HOOR⊦AAAAAAAAAY
Audience: x-xxXXXXXXXX ....

In the fourth example, the applause for Len Murray comes third in a staggered sequence of three displays of approval. As usual, however, it is the one which persists for some time after the others have faded away.

```
(4)  (UK general election, 1979)

Murray:     We need industrial confrontation like we need a
            hole in the head.
Audience:   Hear ⌈hear
Audience:        ⌊Yea ⌈aah ├────────────(8.0)────────────┤
Audience:              ⌊x-xXXXXXXXXXXXXXXXXXXXXXxxx-x
```

Whether or not applause is prompted by some other type of response, it tends to be slower in getting under way than vocal displays of approval. This is because there is an unavoidable time-lag involved in starting to clap one's hands. Shouting 'Hooray', 'Hear hear', or 'Yeah' requires no more preparation than a quick breath of air, whereas hands have to be moved some distance apart before they can be clapped together. And, as people who experiment for themselves will discover, the time it takes to do this is quite long enough for it to be possible to produce a vocal sound before the hands make contact with each other.

Although applause is often not the first response to occur, it regularly wins out in the end against its vocal competitors. One reason why it inevitably takes over is simply that there are physical limits to how much shouting and cheering we can do without running out of breath or becoming hoarse (or both). By comparison, clapping involves no such hazards. It makes no demands whatsoever on our vocal cords, and can therefore be sustained for quite long periods without fear of exhaustion.

A further reason why applause tends to drown out other displays of approval has to do with the way its intensity builds up and persists over time. It gathers strength rather like a wave, and an attempt to depict this has been made in the positioning of the small and large crosses in the transcripts. However, the shape of a typical burst of applause can be perceived more clearly when tape-recordings are fed through electronic equipment originally developed for analysing vocal sounds. The

23

intensity of applause can then be measured and plotted over time, and the shape revealed by this exercise is illustrated by the curve in figure 2.1. This shows that maximum volume is reached within the first second, remains more or less constant for a further five seconds and then falls away slightly more slowly that it built up at the start. Experience suggests that the gentle decline between the 1- and 6-second marks on the graph is inaudible, sounding flatter and more constant than is indicated on the graph. This is because the electronic measuring equipment is more sensitive to slight changes in volume than the human ear. A certain amount of caution is thus required when it comes to interpreting results derived from it, especially when they reveal inconsistencies with the way things actually sound to real people in the real world.

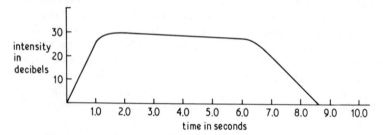

Figure 2.1 Electronic reading of applause intensity

Source: Taken from a PM 200 Pitch and Intensity Analyser manufactured by Voice Identification Inc., Somerville, New Jersey. Equipment made available by kind permission of R.A.W. Bladon, director of the University of Oxford Phonetics Laboratory.

One aspect of the electronically produced picture of applause which is perfectly consistent with the way we hear and talk about applause is the way its intensity rises and falls. The commonly used phrase 'a burst of applause' is thus a remarkably suitable description, in that applause does indeed 'burst' forth very quickly from its point of onset. Similarly, the rather more gradual slope as it comes to an end is aptly reflected in everyday expressions like 'the applause subsided', 'died down' or 'faded away'.

The fact that the intensity of applause reaches its peak so rapidly, and then stays at the same level for some time after that, also has important implications both for public speakers and members of their audiences. It means, for example, that vocal responses have to be produced in the brief period before the clapping reaches maximum intensity if they are to stand a chance of being heard. And from the orator's point of view, there may be considerable advantages if he can time his delivery so that the audience starts to applaud slightly *before* he finishes making a point. This is because an early response will sound much more enthusiastic than one which is delayed until after the speaker has finished what he's saying. One reason for this is that it will look as though members of the audience agreed so strongly with the point being made that they could wait no longer to show their approval. Another is that, by the time the talk actually stops, the applause will already be well on its way to reaching maximum intensity, so that the speaker will appear to have been 'drowned out' by the audience's enthusiasm. An example of this was seen in extract (3), where it appears that Shirley Russell was a very popular choice for the award in question:

---

(3) (British Academy of Film and Television Arts award ceremony, 1980)

Announcer: ...SHIRLEY RUSSE⌐LL FO⌐R YANKS
Audience: └HOOR⊦AAAAAAAAAY
Audience: └x-xxXXXXXXXXX ....

Another point revealed by the electronic reading of the burst of applause depicted in figure 2.1 is that it lasted for about 8.5 seconds. Readers may also have noticed that, in each of the transcribed extracts which showed how long the applause lasted, the timings were very similar. As such, they reflect a general observation that, except at the ends of speeches, when they can go on for very many minutes, bursts of applause show a remarkable and regular tendency to last for seven, eight or nine seconds.

The idea of there being a standardized length of eight seconds (plus or minus one) for bursts of applause may initially seem

2.3 Bursts of applause regularly last for about 8 seconds. So too do the chants of Iranian crowds during speeches by the Ayatollah Khomeini (see also pp. 84–5).

rather bizarre. However, it must be remembered that this observation results directly from the actual behaviour of the thousands of individuals present at the meetings tape-recorded for the purposes of this study. Their behaviour therefore must have been co-ordinated in such a way that the applause regularly came to an end after about eight seconds. And the fact that so many different people on so many different occasions collaborated with each other in clapping for a similar period of time suggests that they must have been operating with some sort of unwritten rule about how much applause is enough.

This orientation to eight seconds as an appropriate length of time for applause to last is not confined to those who are actually involved in doing the clapping. Nor does it apply exclusively to political meetings. In extract (5), for example, the compère had to deal with a situation that is fairly common at show-business award ceremonies. The name of the lucky winner had just been announced, the applause was under way, but there was still no sign of anyone approaching the stage to receive his prize. Under such circumstances, it is the compère's job to intervene with a solution to the problem, and extract (5) is one of many cases where it has been observed that this is done after the audience has been applauding for *eight* seconds.

**(5)   (British Academy of Film and Television Arts
       award ceremony, 1980)**

Audience:	⌈XXXXXXXX⌉ XXXXXXXXxxxxxxxx ⌈xxxxxx-x⌉
Compère:	⌊___(8.0)___⌋Ladies and Gentlemen⌊—(1.2)—⌋
Compère:	like many film actors Robert Duvall is very busy —
	at the moment he's filming in San Francisco ....

The fact that compères routinely wait no more and no less than eight seconds before interrupting means that they decide at just that point that an audience has been clapping long enough, and should be told why the winner has failed to appear. In extract (5) the members of the audience seem to have been quite ready to go along with the compère's assessment of how long is enough, and were quick to respond to 'Ladies and Gentlemen' as a signal to stop clapping. As can be seen, the intensity of their applause had already started to decline by the time the compère was halfway through with her interruption, after which it rapidly faded away.

It appears, then, that both speakers and audiences, in settings as different as political meetings and award ceremonies, are responsive to this unwritten rule that a burst of applause should last for about eight seconds. But rules, of course, can be broken, which raises the question of what happens when the duration of a burst of applause falls outside the 7–9 second range. In other words, if it is regarded as normal to clap for about eight seconds, is it also regarded as *abnormal* to do so for a substantially longer or shorter period of time? The present study suggests that this is probably so, with longer bursts of applause sounding more enthusiastic than normal, and the shorter ones more lukewarm.

In media news reports, for example, an excerpt from a speech is sometimes introduced or referred to as the passage which attracted the most applause from the audience. It is obviously not often possible to get access to tapes of the original speeches in order to check on how long the clapping actually lasted, and so far this has only been done in four such cases. In every one of these, however, it was found that the bursts of applause referred to in the media as 'the longest' or 'most enthusiastic' lasted for *ten or more seconds*, results which are at least consistent with the suggestion that bursts of more than nine seconds are likely to be noticed and reported as being 'longer than normal'.

Comparable evidence on how people regard bursts of applause which last for less than seven seconds is not currently available. However, none of the hundreds of people who have heard tape-recorded examples during lectures on the present study has ever disagreed with the suggestion that these shorter bursts sound feeble and half-hearted in comparison with those falling within the 7–9 second range. It is also something which curious or sceptical readers can readily check for themselves.

The question of how much applause is enough does not arise just when it comes to gauging the enthusiasm of an audience as a whole, but can also become an issue when evaluating the responses of particular individuals and groups within an audience. As the applause gets under way, a politician may be singled out by the zoom lens of a television camera, and this is an ever-present hazard for those who happen to be sitting somewhere alongside the speaker in the front row on the platform. Such close-ups give viewers and commentators an excellent opportunity to scrutinize the amount of vigour with which a person is clapping. Conclusions can then be drawn about an individual's attitude to what has just been said, and about the current state of alliances and divisions within the party more generally. On occasions, politicians caught out in this way are later required to justify or excuse their conduct by television news interviewers, and may even have to face more private interrogation from their party colleagues. As far as is known, however, these have never become as much of a problem for western politicians as they were for Soviet Communist Party members in the 1930s:

At the conclusion of the conference, a tribute to Comrade Stalin was called for. Of course, everyone stood up (just as everyone had leaped to his feet during the conference at every mention of his name).... For three minutes, four minutes, five minutes, the 'stormy applause, rising to an ovation,' continued. But palms were getting sore and raised arms were already aching. And the older people were panting from exhaustion. It was becoming insufferably silly even to those who really adored Stalin. However, who would dare to be the *first* to stop?... After all, NKVD men were standing in the hall applauding and watching to see *who* quit first!... At the rear of the hall, which was crowded, they could of course cheat a bit, clap less frequently, less vigorously, not so eagerly – but up there with the presidium where everyone could see them?... With make-believe enthusiasm on their faces, looking at each other with faint hope, the district leaders were just going on and on applauding till they fell where they stood, till they were carried out of the hall on stretchers!... Then, after eleven minutes, the director of the paper factory assumed a businesslike expression and sat down in his seat. And, oh, a miracle took place! Where had the universal, uninhibited, indescribable enthusiasm gone? To a man, everyone else stopped dead and sat down. They had been saved! The squirrel had been smart enough to jump off his revolving wheel.

That, however, was how they discovered who the indepen-dent people were. And that was how they went about eliminating them. That same night the factory director was arrested. They easily pasted ten years on him on the pretext of something quite different. But after he had signed Form 206, the final document of the interrogation, his interrogator reminded him:

'Don't ever be the first to stop applauding!'
(Alexander Solzhenitsyn, *The Gulag Archipelago*, pp. 69–70)

These dramatic events, of course, took place after the end of a speech, where it is well known that applause can and frequently does last for much more than eight seconds. One reason for this is that there is no question of trespassing on the time available to a speaker once he has finished speaking. Audiences are no longer constrained to give him a chance to continue, and can therefore enter into a much more open-ended commitment to the business of showing their approval. This may partly explain why bursts of applause in the middle of speeches have to be shorter than final ovations, but it does little to resolve the mystery of why they should average out at around the eight-second mark. As far as this is concerned, the best that can be done at present is to offer some highly speculative suggestions.

One relevant factor is that bursts of applause take about a second to reach maximum intensity, and a further two seconds to fade away (see figure 2.1). This means that it is almost impossible for them to last for anything less than three seconds. Our own experiences as audience members also suggest that applause tends to develop an impetus of its own, which somehow propels us into sustaining it for more than another second or two. It is also the case that to do otherwise might imply that we had changed our minds or were less than fully supportive of what had just been said. However, this still leaves open the question of why we tend to stop clapping after about eight seconds.

One extremely speculative solution is suggested by the results of some experiments on short-term memory. From these it emerged that eight seconds may be a critical cut-off point when it comes to remembering certain sorts of things. One set of experiments, for example, involved showing people an obstacle course, after which they were blind-folded and then asked to make their way past the obstacles they had just inspected. The results revealed that those who set off within eight seconds of being blind-folded were more successful in avoiding the obstacles than those whose departure was delayed for more than eight seconds. If this is eventually shown to be a more general feature of short-term memory, it raises the intriguing and amusing possibility that audiences tend to stop clapping when they do because, by the time the critical eight seconds have elapsed, they have forgotten what had prompted them to applaud in the first place.

Response timing

The duration and intensity of applause are not the only features of it that remain remarkably constant across a large number of instances. There is also a great deal of regularity in the way audiences co-ordinate their behaviour with that of public speakers. As was noted earlier, people do not just clap and cheer whenever they feel like it, but do so only at specific points in the course of the proceedings. Indeed, this is what was so successfully exploited when the curtain failed to come down at the end of *The Bed-Sitting Room*, and is also a major reason for the embarrassment felt by those who start clapping in the wrong place at a concert. However, the fact that such hitches are comparatively rare means that it must be more usual for audiences to have no problems at all in knowing exactly when they should or should not produce a burst of applause.

There are two senses, at least, in which it can be said that there are right and wrong places for audiences to show their approval, and both are important if we are to understand how public speakers and audiences communicate with each other. The first has to do with the way responses are timed to fit in with where a speaker has got to in delivering a message: at what precise points do audiences actually interrupt the flow of talk from the platform? And the second concerns the positioning of displays of approval in relation to the contents of a speech: what sorts of messages do audiences deem to be worthy of applause?

With regard to the question of timing, audiences appear to be continually on the look-out for suitable completion points in the talk where applause can occur. The most obvious of these is, of course, when a whole speech comes to an end. However, in the course of any speech, there are plenty of other more temporary completion points where audiences have opportunities for showing their approval. These most commonly occur when the speaker sums up the gist of an argument before developing a related point or moving to a new topic. Applause thus regularly occurs at the end of a flow of talk which is approximately equivalent to a paragraph of written text. In extract (6), for example, Neil Kinnock follows up a series of rhetorical questions with an answer summing up his position on all of them (arrowed). The audience starts to applaud just before he reaches completion.

---

(6) (Labour Party conference, 1983)

Kinnock: Are our senior citizens in Britain being suffocated by a pension from November of thirty four pounds and five p a week? I ask, are the seven million of our countrymen and women being suffocated by their supplementary benefits? I ask if the young people who in this country are lucky enough to get on the youth training scheme are being suffocated by the paltry twenty five pounds a week? Are their unemployed contemporaries being suffocated by the fifteen and sixteen and seventeen pounds a week, soon to be cut according to the government? I say that these people are not being suffocated by care, they are being smothered by neglect, by the contempt of a cruel government

Audience: x-xxX̲X̲XXXXXXXXXXXXXXXXXXXXXXX ....

The precision with which audiences time their responses becomes more evident when one considers where applause tends to occur in the course of an actual sentence. Thus, in all the extracts seen so far, the responses started close to the end of

32

a sentence. As further examples are introduced, it will be seen that this is a common feature of the way audiences time their displays of approval: in the vast majority of cases, these begin to get under way either just before or immediately after the speaker reaches such a completion point. By contrast, instances like extract (7), where there was a whole second's delay before the audience started to applaud Peter Shore, are very few and far between:

---

(7) (UK general election, 1979)

Shore: ... it's one thing to sell to sitting tenants, and it's quite another to keep houses empty while they're hawked around to find some purchaser who could just as well buy in the open market like any other owner occupier does.
(1.0-second silence)
⊢————(5.0)————⊣
Audience: -x- (0.2) -x-xx-xxxxxxxxx-xx-x

From the professional politician's point of view, it is probably fortunate that delays like this do not happen too frequently, because just as responses which start earlier than usual tend to sound exceptionally enthusiastic (see extract 3), so too do those which start later than usual tend to sound exceptionally reluctant or hesitant. Nor is delay the only factor that can make a burst of applause sound half-hearted, as what happens after it starts also provides a basis for making negative evaluations. The way the applause gets under way, or rather fails to do so, in extract (7) is fairly typical of what tends to occur when a response starts after a gaping silence has begun to open up: it starts off more spasmodically than usual, fails to reach full intensity and then fizzles out after a meagre five seconds have elapsed. The combined effect of all this is a response which sounds so hesitant, feeble and lukewarm that it may well leave an even more damaging impression than if no one had applauded at all.

If displays of approval are seldom delayed for more than a split second after a completion point, and frequently start just before one is reached, it means that speakers must be supplying their audiences with advance notice as to precisely *when* they should start clapping. Otherwise, it is quite impossible to see how anyone would ever be able to respond so promptly, and silences of the sort which greeted Peter Shore in extract (7) would be much more common. The fact is, however, that audiences are very skilled at anticipating exactly when applause is due. They must therefore be able not just to recognize cues or instructions embedded within the talk, but to do so soon enough to be ready to respond by the time a completion point is reached. And if audiences can identify such instructions on a single hearing, observers should be able to do the same from tape-recordings of speeches. From the privileged vantage point of viewers with access to action replays, it should also be possible to obtain a fuller understanding of how such sequences work than was available to those who actually produced the bursts of applause in the first place.

The main verbal and non-verbal methods for inviting applause are described in chapter 3. However, the types of message which routinely attract applause play an important part in the process. It is therefore necessary first to consider the second of our two questions about the timing of displays of approval, namely what sorts of messages do audiences deem to be worthy of applause?

Applaudable messages

'Let us now show our appreciation in the usual manner' is a particularly blunt instrument for getting an audience to start clapping, but it is also an extremely efficient one. As such, it exhibits characteristics which feature more widely in the sort of talk that precedes applause, but which are often less obviously apparent.

In the first place, by calling for a display of appreciation, the speaker makes an *evaluative assessment*, in this case of the person or persons being thanked. Secondly, by calling for it 'now', he informs the audience that he has *no further* compliments or congratulations to offer, and hence that there will be nothing to stop them from echoing his sentiments as soon as he has finished this particular announcement. Thirdly, by calling on 'us' to show 'our' appreciation, the speaker claims to be representing the collective mood, and to be speaking *on behalf of* the audience as a whole. The message is thus constructed in such a way as to leave those present in no doubt whatsoever about what to do next. And, as can be seen from the actual examples throughout this book (or by looking at others), these three properties are common to most, if not all, sequences of talk to which audiences respond with a collective display of approval.

If certain types of message are more likely than others to be treated as 'applaudable', anyone in the audience who notices that a politician has launched into the delivery of such a message will thus be alerted to pay close attention to what follows so as to be ready to applaud at the first possible opportunity.

Favourable references to persons

A first type of message which is used in a wide variety of public settings in addition to political meetings involves favourable references to persons, like the one just discussed. They are typically found at the beginnings and endings of speeches, and at other transitional points in the proceedings, and are used for performing various standardized (but none the less important) tasks like marking the end of a speech or introducing the next speaker. Examples of speakers doing both these things can be seen in extract (8):

---

(8) (Conservative Party conference, 1978)

Speaker: ... I beg to support the motion.
          ┝———————(8.0)————————┥
Audience: x-xxXXXXXXXXxxx-x
Chair: Now it's my pleasure to invite Mr Michael Heseltine, the Member of Parliament for Henley, Shadow Minister of the Environment, to reply to the debate.
          Mist⌈er Heseltine┝————(9.0)————————————┥
Audience: ⌊ x-xx-xxXXXXXXXXXXXXXXXXXXXXXxx-x

Very similar introductory messages are also used in quite different settings, as is illustrated by the following example from a show-business award ceremony:

---

(9) (British Academy of Film and Television Arts award ceremony, 1980)

Compère: The British Academy recognizes the importance of children's television with the Rediffusion Star Awards. To tell us about them we are fortunate to have with us tonight the Minister for the Arts, the Right Honourable Mr Norman St John-Stevas.

              ├─────(9.0)─────┤

Audience: x-x-xxXXXXXXXXXXXxx-x

Applause also routinely follows when someone is being commended or congratulated by a speaker, and extracts (10) and (11) again provide illustrations from the same two contrasting settings:

---

(10) (Conservative Party conference, 1980)

Thatcher: I am however very fortunate in having a marvellous deputy, who's wonderful in all places, at all times, in all things,

             Willie White⌈law ├─────(8.0)─────┤

Audience: ⌊x-xxXXXXXXXXXXXxxx-x

---

(11) (British Academy of Film and Television Arts award ceremony, 1980)

*Presenter: Congratulations.

*Winner: ⌈Thank you├─────(8.0)─────┤

Audience: ⌊x-xx-xxXXXXXXXXXXXXXXXXXXXXXXxxx-x

(*Speakers appearing on large TV monitor at the rear of the stage.)

In this last example, the fact that the actual presentation is taking place 6000 miles away and is being beamed to the audience on a giant television screen has no effect on their ability either to produce a very prompt burst of applause (which actually coincides with the verbal response of the winner) or to sustain it for a full eight seconds.

When speakers make pleasant remarks about the person they are introducing or commending, they are doing something which stands a very good chance of being approved of by their audience. This is because such activities usually involve them not just in making a personal statement of appreciation, but in expressing the collective sentiment of the assembled multitude as a whole. As Mrs Thatcher's deputy, for example, Mr Whitelaw is also deputy leader of the entire Conservative Party. If he is deserving of gratitude from her, then he presumably also deserves it from the party at large. It is therefore very likely that the audience at a party conference will feel inclined to endorse their leader's glowing tribute. By praising the party's deputy leader, Mrs Thatcher was thus able to catch the mood of the audience with a positive evaluation that is readily recognizable by everybody as being 'on behalf of us all'.

Favourable references to 'us'

Another type of message which regularly attracts a favourable audience response involves directing praise not just to a particular individual, but to 'us' in general. Thus, assertions which convey positive or boastful evaluations of our hopes, our activities or our achievements stand a very good chance of being endorsed by audiences with a burst of applause.

It appears that this applies quite independently of who 'we' happen to be. In extracts (12) and (13) for example, two US presidents use 'we' to speak boastfully on behalf of an entire nation:

---

(12) (Inaugural address as US president, 1961)

Kennedy: We shall pay any price, bear any burden, meet any hardship, support any friend, oppose any foe, to assure the survival and success of liberty.

Audience: xxXXXXXXX (TV editor's cut after 2.0 seconds)

---

(13)   (Inaugural address as US president, 1981)

Reagan: Those who are potential adversaries, they will be
             reminded that peace is the highest aspiration of
             the American people. We will negotiate for it,
             sacrifice for it, we will not surrender for it now or
             ever.

             |————————————————(11.0)————————————————|
Audience: x-x-xx-XXXXXXXXXXXXXXXXXXXXXXXxx-xx-x

Applause may also follow boastful claims about the aims and achievements of governments which have already been in power for a few years, as in the following excerpts from speeches made by two British prime ministers fighting elections while still in office:

(14)   (UK general election, 1979)

Callaghan: There's work for a Labour Government for the
             next five years, as long as there's a family
             without a home, as long as there's a patient
             waiting in a queue for a hospital bed, as long as
             there's a man or a woman without a job,
             someone who suffers from discrimination be-
             cause of their colour; so long will our work as a
             Labour movement not be done. We go forward
             in that spirit, and with that resolve.
Audience: xxXXXXXXXXX (TV editor's cut after 3.0
             seconds)

(2)   (UK general election, 1983)

Thatcher: There's no government anywhere that is tackling
             the problem with more vigour, imagination and
             determination than this Conservative govern-
             ment.
Audience: Hear ⌈hear |————————————(8.0)————————————|
Audience: ⌊ xxXXXXXXXXXXXXXXXXXXXXXXXXxxx-x

When spokesmen for minority groups or political parties make positive evaluations of 'us', they are likely, for obvious reasons, to relate to aims and hopes for the future, as can be seen in excerpts from speeches by the late Martin Luther King, black American civil rights leader, and David Steel and Roy Jenkins of the British Liberal and Social Democratic parties respectively:

---

(15) (Speech to striking garbage-workers, Memphis, 1968)

King: ... but I want you to know tonight that we
            as a people will get to the promised
            lan⌐d
Audience: ⌊Yea⌐hh ├————————(7.5)——————————┤
Audience: ⌊ xxXXXXXXXXXXXXXXXXXXXXXXXXxxx-x

(16) (UK general election, 1983)

Steel: This is a great day for us because it's the day on
            which the Liberal–Alliance campaign is really
            taking off across the country.
Audience: Hoo⌐raaaaay
Audience: ⌊xxXXXXXXXXX (TV editor's cut after 1.5
            seconds)

(17) (Liberal Party assembly, 1982)

Jenkins: Our aim is to win seats, not just fight them.
Audience: ├————————(8.0)————————┤
Audience: x-xxXXXXXXXXXXXXXxxx-x

Praiseworthy evaluations of 'our side' involve speakers in comparing 'us' favourably with 'them'. If 'we' are virtuous, resolute and full of good intentions, then presumably 'they' must be wicked, weak and full of bad intentions. However, insults aimed at 'them' do not have to be left implicit, but can and often do comprise the main burden of a politician's message. When made openly, criticisms and attacks directed at opponents also have a similar capacity for attracting a favourable response, and as such constitute another important type of applaudable message.

The fact that messages which are hostile towards 'them' regularly win favour with audiences is, of course, not particularly surprising. It is widely known that the need to resist an external threat, whether real or imagined, has always been an extremely effective rallying cry when it comes to strengthening group solidarity and morale. Politicians have never been slow to exploit the potential of being able to present their audiences with a bogeyman, who can be depicted as the 'real enemy' on whom all 'our' troubles can be blamed. Such a strategy was pursued relentlessly and with spectacular results by Adolf Hitler. And although the rise of Nazism and the ensuing holocaust may be an extreme example of where a sustained campaign of insults can lead, it is none the less an important reminder of how remarkably responsive and vulnerable audiences can be to messages of this type.

Minority groups are obviously only one of a very large number of possible targets that can be singled out for attack. Entire countries and political systems are often subjected to a barrage of insults by politicians, and attacks on the opposing power bloc have become part and parcel of the rhetoric of the cold war. They are also likely to be met with a favourable audience response, as in the following excerpt from a speech by Mrs Thatcher.

---

(18)   (Conservative Party conference, 1980)

Thatcher: Soviet marxism is ideologically, politically, and
             morally bankru⌐pt ⊢————————(9.0)————————⊣
Audience: ⌊xxXXXXXXXXXXXXXXXXXXxx-x

In countries where different political parties are allowed to operate, there is always a ready supply of local targets, and insults aimed at rival parties can be relied on to find favour with audiences. Sometimes, as in extract (19), a boast from the other side can be turned into an insult, and redirected back to its point of origin:

```
(19)  (UK general election, 1979)

Heath:       ... the Labour Prime Minister and his colleagues
             are boasting in this election campaign that they
             have brought inflation down from the disastrous
             level of twenty six per cent. But we are entitled to
             inquire who put it up to twenty six per cent?
Audience:    Heh ┌heh├───────────(8.0)────────────┤
Audience:        └x-xxXXXXXXXXXXXXXXXXXXXXXXXXxx-x
```

While the two major parties tend to concentrate their attacks
on each other, members of minority or centre parties in the
middle of the political spectrum treat both of them as equally
eligible targets for their insults. In extract (20), for example, the
Liberal Party leader launches a simultaneous attack on the
Labour and Conservative parties:

```
(20)  (UK general election, 1979)

Steel:       ... there are two conservative parties in this
             election. One is offering the continuation of the
             policies we've had for the last five years, and the
             other is offering a return to the policies of forty
             years a┌go
Audience:           └Heh h┌eh heh├─────────(8.0)──────────┤
Audience:                 └ xXXXXXXXXXXXXXXXXXXxxx-x
```

Disputes within the British Labour Party between the 1979
and 1983 general elections involved frequent attacks by its
members on targets selected from within their own ranks. In
1980, only a few months before the Social Democrats broke
away to form their own party, one memorable insult aimed at
the Labour MPs who were then thinking of doing so attracted a
very enthusiastic reception at the party's annual conference. For
this, former prime minister James Callaghan received a *twelve-*
second ovation. The excerpt was subsequently replayed on all
the main television news programmes later that day, and the
slogans 'Dead as a dodo' and 'Mere fluff' were widely featured
in the following day's newspaper headlines.

Meanwhile, Mr Callaghan himself was at the receiving end of insults from the left of the Labour Party at the same annual conference. Extract (22) is the finale of a speech by his former cabinet colleague, Mr Tony Benn, in which Callaghan and the party leadership were accused of having behaved undemocratically in deciding what policy proposals to include in the party's manifesto for the election they had just lost. In this case Mr Benn's supporters in the audience could not wait for him to end with a standardized conclusion, and started to clap even before the final insult was fully complete.

The left wing of the Labour Party also came in for its fair share of insults from rival factions within the party, and one of the most famous of these was Mr Denis Healey's reference to them as 'Toytown Trotskies'. Although this was widely taken up by the media, it actually misfired rather badly with at least one of the audiences to which it was addressed. Just as he was coming to the completion point, when those who agreed with him would normally have started clapping, an intervention from the chair informed him over the public-address system that his time was up. It was then this utterance, rather than Mr Healey's, which received favourable audience responses:

---

(23)   (Labour Party special conference, May 1980)

Healey: ... we won't do it if instead of meeting the real needs of the British people we go on ideological ego trips, or accept the clapped out dogmas which are now being trailed by the Toytown Trotskies of the militant grou⌈p.

Lady Jeger: ⌊Denis – five minutes for ev⌈erybody.

Audience: ⌊Yeahhh⌈hhhhhhhhhhhhhhhhhhhhhhhhhh ....

Audience: ⌊x-xxXX⌈XXXXXXXXXXXXXX ....

Healey: ⌊What we've got to do ....

The displays of approval for Lady Jeger's intervention thus started before she had finished, and had already reached maximum intensity before Mr Healey could get a chance to continue. As a result, he was left struggling to make himself heard above the combined noise of a roar of agreement and loud applause which, taken together, left little doubt that the audience was well pleased with the chair's attempt to silence him.

Given that audiences regularly applaud in response to a boast about 'us' or an insult aimed at 'them', it is hardly surprising that the same applies when a speaker manages to do both at once. An example of this can be seen in extract (24), where Liberal leader David Steel used the results of a newspaper survey of election manifestoes to compare the Conservative and Labour parties unfavourably with his own.

```
┌─────────────────────────────────────────────────────────────┐
│  (24)  (UK general election, 1979)                          │
│                                                              │
│  Steel:       You know when the Guardian newspaper looked   │
│               through the manifestoes last week for new ideas,│
│               they awarded us forty two points, against      │
│               Labour's eleven and the Tories' nine.          │
│  Audience:    Heh heh ⌈heh ┝━━━━━━━━(7.0)━━━━━━━━┥           │
│  Audience:           └ x-xxXXXXXXXXXXXXXXXXXXXXxxx-x          │
└─────────────────────────────────────────────────────────────┘
```

Here, as in extract (20), Mr Steel can be seen to be practising
something that he has frequently preached against, namely 'Yah
boo politics'. This phrase has been widely used by Liberals and
Social Democrats to refer to what they regard as a major
disadvantage of a political system in which the two leading
parties continually throw insults at each other, a situation
which they claim would be radically changed if only more
people would vote for a third party grouping. However, as we
have already seen, more dispassionate observation clearly
shows that politicians of *all* political persuasions make extensive use of messages which amount to saying 'Yah boo' to their
opponents. Nor is it particularly surprising that they do so in
view of the fact that insults aimed at 'them' can be so regularly
relied on to attract favourable responses from audiences.

The same applies equally to boastful evaluations of 'us' and
more standardized welcomes to and commendations of persons.
As was seen in extracts (6)–(17), they too are messages which
are widely used by politicians of all shades of opinion, and
which are regularly followed by bursts of applause. A general
conclusion to be drawn from all this is that audience displays of
approval tend only to occur in response to a narrow range of
very simple types of political message. The ones most frequently followed by applause are those where the speaker in effect
says either 'Hooray for *us*' or 'Yah boo to *them*'. A statistically
adequate estimate of their relative frequency has yet to be
arrived at, and is likely to reveal significant variations between
different speakers and different types of political meeting.
However, a count of the messages which preceded 100 bursts of
applause during speeches at party conferences yielded the
figures shown in table 2.1. From this it can be seen that eighty-

four bursts of applause occurred in response to positive evaluations of 'us', negative evaluations of 'them' or some combination of the two. And more than 9 out of 10 cases (95 per cent) were responsive to one or other of the message types described here.

Table 2.1	Distribution of message types occurring before 100 bursts of applause at British political party conferences

message type	number
Positive evaluation of 'us'	40
Negative evaluation of 'them'	34
Combined positive and negative evaluation	10
Standardized introduction, commendation, etc.	11
Other	5
total	100

Organized spontaneity

On close examination, 'showing our appreciation in the usual manner' can be seen to be a much more regular, finely timed and precisely co-ordinated form of behaviour than it appears at first sight. Audiences typically start clapping just after vocal displays of approval like 'Hear hear', 'Yeah' and 'Hooray', which are then usually drowned out by the rising intensity of the applause. With one or two notable exceptions, which are considered in more detail later, speakers respond by waiting for the applause to die away before making any attempt to continue. By so doing, they implicitly acknowledge that a display of approval is indeed an appropriate thing for the audience to be doing at that particular point in the proceedings. Audience members also tend to collaborate with each other in clapping with a similar degree of intensity and for similar periods of time, the average duration being around eight seconds. And the vast majority of such responses are timed to occur just before or just after a speaker completes the delivery of one of a very limited range of rather simple types of message.

Professional politicians would no doubt prefer us to think of displays of approval as wholly spontaneous responses to the depth and wisdom of their words. Unfortunately, however, the available evidence provides few grounds for so doing. And, as was mentioned earlier, it is easy enough for anyone with a radio or television set to check on the validity of these conclusions for themselves.

Compared with boasts and insults, standardized messages like 'Let us now show our appreciation in the usual manner' convey more explicit instructions as to when an audience should start clapping. But this does not mean that messages like boasts and insults are devoid of any such instructions, for they too have to be packaged and delivered in a way which informs the audience *that* they should respond favourably, as well as exactly *when* they should start doing so. Indeed, the fact that they regularly time their responses to coincide so closely with the completion of any particular message suggests that there must be something else about the talk that enables them to come in 'on cue'.

In addition to considering the sorts of messages that regularly prompt audiences to applaud, it is therefore important to look just as closely at how politicians *package* and *deliver* these messages in such a way as to leave people in no doubt as to when they should start clapping. When this is done, it emerges that there is also a great deal of regularity about the forms of words, rhythm, volume, intonation and non-verbal actions used by speakers and recognized by audiences as pointers to the place where applause should begin. What these are and how they work are considered in the next chapter.

English Dictionary, is 'a trick, device, or language designed to catch applause'. As such, it provides a very apt description of the techniques of the orator's trade examined in this chapter.

In the interests of clarity, it is necessary to look at these one by one, but it is important to stress from the outset that the successful claptrap always involves the use of more than one technique at a time. This is because of the difficulties involved in co-ordinating the activities of a large number of individuals, not all of whom can be relied on to be paying full attention to what a speaker is saying. To resolve such problems, an orator has to communicate with his audience in much the same way as a conductor communicates with an orchestra or choir. A single movement of the hand, arm, head, lips or eyes is unlikely to be enough to get musicians to come in on time. They may not all be equally attentive, and some of them will not have a sufficiently good view of the conductor to be able to notice one isolated signal on its own. But if he waves his baton, nods his head, and mouths the word 'Now!', synchronizing them all to occur at the same time, the chances of everyone spotting at least one of them are greatly increased. Because each different move conveys an identical message, none of the musicians should be in any doubt as to what to do and when to do it. In the same way, an effective claptrap must provide audience members with a number of signals which make it quite clear both *that* they should applaud and *when* they should start doing so.

This is partially achieved by the content of what an orator says. As was seen in the previous chapter, once the audience notices that an introduction, commendation, boast or insult is under way, they can get ready to start clapping at the first possible completion point. But such messages have to be packaged in a way which deals with two potential sources of difficulty for those in the audience. In the first place, the speaker must make it quite clear to them that he has launched into the final stage of delivering an applaudable message. Secondly, he has to supply enough advance information for them to be able to anticipate the precise point at which the message will be completed. So long as both these things are done, audiences can be led through the first two stages of the type of sequence exemplified by 'Hip, hip – Hooray!' and 'On your marks, get set – Go!' And once they have committed themselves to participating in such a process there is little to stop them from coming in on cue.

Because a successful claptrap has to be built up through several phases, orators need to have a very good sense of timing. To see how the whole process works, it is therefore essential to take note of which words are stressed more than others, and where speakers pause in the course of their delivery. These additional details are included in the transcripts which follow. Stressed words or parts of words are underlined, and passages of louder talk than usual are printed in capital letters. All pauses have been timed to the nearest tenth of a second, and are indicated by numbers in brackets. A micro-pause lasting less than two-tenths of a second is shown as a dot between brackets.

Projecting a name

The workings of a successful claptrap can be seen most clearly by looking first at the more ritualized forms of messages, such as introductions and commendations. By far and away the commonest way of delivering these is to identify the person in question ('On your marks'), say a few words about him ('Get set') and then name him ('Go!'). The audience is thus given time to realize that this is something to be applauded, to anticipate what name will signal completion and to get ready to start clapping as soon as they hear it. In extracts (8) and (10), the speakers helped the process along by pausing briefly just before finally announcing the projected names. And in each case, the audiences had no difficulty in getting the applause under way before the names were fully out.

---

(8)   (Conservative Party conference, 1978)

Chair: Now it's my pleasure to (.) in<u>vi</u>te Mister Michael
              Heseltine the Member of Parliament for Henley
              (0.2) Shadow Minister of the Environment to
              reply to the de<u>bate</u>.
              (0.2)
              <u>Mist</u>⌈er Heseltine ⊢————————(9.0)————————⊣
Audience: ⌊x-xx-xxXXXXXXXXXXXXXXXXXXXXXxx-x

---

(10) (Conservative Party conference, 1980)

Thatcher: I am however (0.2) very fortunate (0.4) in having
(0.6) a <u>mar</u>vellous deputy (0.4) who's wonderful
(.) in <u>all</u> places (0.2) at all times (0.2) in all things.
(0.2)
Willie White⌐law ⊦————————(8.0)————————⊦
Audience: ⌐x-xxXXXXXXXXXXXXXXXXxxx-x

The use of words like 'now' and 'however' is extremely
common at the beginning of such sequences. This is because
they provide speakers with a simple and economical way of
signalling to the audience that they are launching into something different from what was going on previously. And that
something might, of course, turn out to be calling for additional
attention, and perhaps even applause. In these two examples,
the fact that the message to be delivered is indeed one which
should be applauded is quickly communicated. If the conference chairman has 'pleasure' and Mrs Thatcher is 'very fortunate', the audience is likely to share such sentiments and hence
be willing to display them with a round of applause. That an
applaudable message is under way is then progressively confirmed, first by the identification of popular figures within the
Conservative Party, and then with the addition of a few words
about them. Once this has been done, all that remains is for the
speakers to give the go-ahead: an applaudable message has been
delivered, a completion point has been clearly projected, and
the audience has been given plenty of time to get ready to clap
on hearing the name.

Members of audiences are not the only people who regularly
recognize and act upon signals which project a completion
point. The same cues are also used by television production
staff for making decisions about when to switch from one
camera to another. For example, when extract (10) was shown
on television, the close-up shot of Mrs Thatcher was replaced by
one of a beaming Mr Whitelaw when she was halfway through
saying his surname. This is illustrated by the picture sequence
in plate 3.1, where it can be seen that the image being screened
was switched from Mrs Thatcher to Mr Whitelaw at precisely

3.1 Audience and television production staff respond on cue as Mrs Thatcher commends her deputy (extract 10).

'... Willie ...'

'... White- ...'

'... law.'

the same moment as the first clap came from the audience. The person responsible for deciding which picture to transmit to viewers was therefore presumably responding to exactly the same signals as those which prompted the audience to start clapping.

It is not always the case that the person to be named is identified in quite so straightforward a manner as was done in extracts (8) and (10). Speakers sometimes only hint at who it is, and leave the audience to guess his identity. This procedure can work perfectly well so long as the audience is given enough time to solve the puzzle before the delivery of the name is completed. In extract (25), for example, the compère pauses after giving the clues, delays further with 'Ladies and Gentlemen' and then pauses again. The stressed first name and the micro-pause before the surname subsequently give the audience another opportunity to anticipate a name which will link 'Kenneth' to the information they already have:

---

(25)　(British Academy of Film and Television Arts award ceremony, 1980)

Compère:　Here to read the nominations is a man (0.7) who seems to lead another life on video, a life (0.3) so bizarre and way out that if he didn't exist (0.4) we wouldn't know how to invent him.
　　　(0.4)
　　　Ladies and Gentlemen,
　　　(0.2)
　　　Mister <u>Kenneth</u>
　　　(.)
　　　Everett.

Audience:　⌈(whistle)⊢————(9.0)————⊣

Audience:　⌊x-xxXXXXXXXXXXXXXXXXXXXXXXXXxx-x

By the time the surname is delivered, enough details have been provided to enable anyone familiar with British television personalities to come up with the right answer. In spite of having been given extra time, however, the audience still cannot manage to start clapping quite as early as in the previous cases, where there was no doubt at all that Messrs Heseltine and Whitelaw were the people about to be named.

A variation of this guessing game is also often used for announcing the names of winners at award ceremonies. In the following excerpts, a speaker reads out the names of a number of nominees from whom one will be selected as the winner. In effect, this instructs the audience to start clapping on hearing any *one* of the names listed.

---

(5)   (British Academy of Film and Television Arts award ceremony, 1980)

Announcer: The best supporting actor (0.7) the nominations are (0.5) Robert Duvall (0.4) for Apocalypse Now (0.5) Denholm Elliot (0.4) for Saint Jack (0.8) John Hurt (0.8) for Alien (0.8) Christopher Walken (1.0) for The Deer Hunter.
(1.8)
The winner is
(0.8)
Robert Duvaₗll (0.5) for Apocalypse Now

Audience: ˪x-xxxxxxxxxxxXXXXXXXXXX . . . .

---

(26)   (British Academy of Film and Television Arts awards ceremony, 1980)

Announcer: The best supporting actress (0.4) the nominations are (0.4) Lisa Eichorn (0.4) for The Europeans (0.6) Mariel Hemingway (0.4) for Manhattan (0.6) Rachel Roberts (0.4) for Yanks (0.4) Meryl Streep (0.4) for Manhattan.
(1.4)
And the winner is
(1.4)
RACHEL ROBERTS FOR ⌜YANKS ⊢——(9.0)——⊣

Audience: ˪x-xxXXXXXXXXxxx-x

53

In these cases, the pauses before the final naming tend to be much longer than in the earlier examples. This is because the name of the lucky winner is concealed inside an envelope, and more time is therefore taken up as the announcer struggles to open it. Meanwhile, the audience has been placed in a position where there is absolutely no doubt that applause will be due as soon as the news is out: they know *that* and *when* they should start clapping, but have to hold back for however long it takes to open the envelope and read out the name. A very simple procedure thus operates as an extremely effective way of building up suspense.

It can be seen that the actual announcements of who won continue some way beyond the point where the name becomes recognizable. Repeating the name of the film after the name of the person provides extra time for the audience to get their response under way *before* completion is finally reached. The chances of a pause opening up and the audience response being interpreted as insufficiently enthusiastic is therefore minimized. As will be seen later, a pause just before getting to completion and a slightly extended final segment of talk are both common features in the design of most types of claptrap. The pause gives the audience a last chance to anticipate the projected completion point, and the additional beats provide space for them not just to start clapping, but to do so early enough to avoid the possibility of an embarrassing silence between the end of the talk and the beginning of the applause.

The fundamental importance of projecting a clearly recognizable completion point can best be seen by looking at what happens when a speaker gets it all wrong. In extract (27), the then minister for the arts, Mr Norman St John-Stevas, starts by announcing that three awards are about to be made, but then goes straight on to declare the first result *without* supplying a preliminary list of nominees, as had been done in a long series of previous announcements like those in extracts (5) and (26). The strategy misfires rather badly, with a deathly silence opening up at the very point (arrowed in the transcript) where the audience should have responded:

On naming the winner and the programme, nothing happens for 1.5 seconds. The unfortunate Mr St John-Stevas then responds to the absence of applause by starting to announce the winner of the next award. As he does so, the audience realizes what he is doing, and sees the opportunity to show approval for the first award fast disappearing. Accordingly, they begin to clap, and Stevas promptly defers to them by stopping in his tracks. Two and a half seconds later, by which time the applause is well under way, he can then be heard apologizing to the compère. By so doing, he acknowledges not only that something has gone wrong, but also that it was his fault. What happens when he does eventually continue to the second award, however, is quite different:

Things get progressively better for Mr St John-Stevas as the audience adapts to the fact that he is using another kind of claptrap involving no preliminary list of nominees. After the second winner is announced, they are already able to start clapping immediately on completion of the name of the programme. And on the third occasion they manage to come in after the name of the winner, which is exactly the same position at which they had been responding in the earlier examples.

In a very similar case at a Conservative Party conference, Mr James Prior, who was then the employment minister, made the mistake of trying to commend three people at once without first going through the preliminary phases of identification and description. After making it quite clear that he was about to commend his colleagues, he went straight ahead and named them. When nothing happened, he pointed them out and informed the audience where the people in question were to be seen on the platform, a move which made it look as though he was specifically holding them up for public acclaim there and then. The audience finally managed to produce a rather brief and hesitant response, only to be told by Mr Prior that they were not supposed to have started clapping yet:

---

(28) (Conservative Party conference, 1980)

Prior: And that is to say (0.2) how much I value the support (0.4) and the advice that I've had (0.2) from Grey Gowrie, Jim Lester and Patrick Mayhew (0.2)

who are sitting on my right here |———(5.0)———|

Audience: x-xx-xxxxxx-x-x

Prior: Yes, I don't want you to clap too early because I want just to say another word about each of them ...

'I don't want you to clap too early' is the only example observed so far where a politician openly admits not just that there are proper places for audiences to applaud, but that he will be wanting them to do so in due course. It is also apparent that Mr Prior knows how such sequences ought in principle to be organized, even though he failed so dismally to put the theory into practice: by noting that the audience response should be deferred until after he has said 'another word about each of them', he acknowledges that the identification and descriptive remarks should have been delivered *before* the final naming of the persons being commended (as in the more effectively executed examples seen earlier).

For public speakers, the lesson of all this is clear: if a claptrap is to work smoothly, it has to be carefully built up through a series of distinct phases as in 'On your marks, get set – Go!' The steps taken must therefore ensure that the audience is given enough advance information and enough time to be able both to recognize that the message calls for applause and to anticipate when it will be completed.

Although naming someone who has already been identified is an efficient enough claptrap to use when announcing prize-winners, or introducing or commending another person, it is obviously not a very versatile way of packaging boasts about 'us' or insults aimed at 'them'. For these purposes, other verbal formats are required, and there are two which are particularly widely used in political speeches: in a large proportion of cases, applause occurs after a speaker has produced either a list or a contrast (or some combination of the two).

Lists of three

In speeches, conversations and most other forms of communication, the most commonly used type of list contains *three* items, and an example of such a list has just been used to start this sentence. One of the main attractions of three-part lists is that they have an air of unity or completeness about them. Lists comprising only two items tend to appear inadequate or incomplete – so much so that there are various phrases that can be slotted in whenever we are having difficulty in finding a suitable third item for a list. The phrase 'and other forms of communication', the third item in the above list, is thus fairly typical of the sort of vague and unimaginative improvisations we regularly resort to under such circumstances. Others include 'and so on', 'somethingorother', 'thingummyjig', 'what-chumacallit' and 'etcetera'. On their own, they are empty categories which do not refer to anything directly, and their main function seems to be to provide us with an all-purpose and readily available solution to the problem of completing a list. And one widely used three-part list – 'this, that and the other' – is made up entirely of this sort of category.

Stronger evidence that lists with three items tend to be regarded as complete comes from research into conversational communication. This shows that speakers who embark on producing a list often get stuck after a second item, and only manage to continue as far as 'and uh—'. Relatively long pauses frequently follow at such points, and what is particularly interesting is that these silences are seldom exploited by potential next speakers as an opportunity to start talking. If people are prepared to wait patiently until a speaker finds something to put into the third slot, it means that they must be acknowledging that the utterance has not yet been properly completed. However, if someone is foolhardy enough to try producing a list with four or more parts to it, there is a very high risk of his being interrupted. And the commonest place for such interruptions to occur is immediately after the completion of the *third* item in a list.

Just as third items in lists are widely regarded as possible completion points in conversational communication, so too are they treated as completion points at which audience responses can occur at political meetings. A simple example of this is provided by the way chanting is commonly organized, as is illustrated in extracts (29) and (30). Here, opponents and supporters of Mrs Thatcher begin their chants all together and *immediately* after the lone voice in the crowd has completed the third 'Maggie'. Then, just as promptly, the cheer-leaders come in again as soon as the crowds complete the third 'out' and 'in'. By orienting to third items as completion points, crowds are thus able to keep such sequences going for quite some time.

---

(29) (UK general election, 1983)

Lone voice:	Maggie – Maggie – Maggie –
Crowd:	– Out – out – out –
Lone voice:	– Maggie – Maggie – Maggie –
Crowd:	– Out – out – out –

The fact that people tend to treat the completion of the third item in a list as the point where a next utterance should begin is also important for the smooth running of other types of sequence where some utterance has to be produced in unison. In church services, for example, members of the congregation have few problems in saying 'Amen' together after a priest has said 'the Father, the Son and the Holy Ghost'. And even where less familiar prayers are involved, a three-part structure can help them to come in on time. Thus, in the following example they are instructed what they should say, but not how they will know when a prayer has finished. After the first prayer, the vicar has to prompt them, but when the second one comprises three similar elements, the congregation is able to come in much earlier and without any further assistance from the vicar:

---

(31) (Church of England, Evensong)

Vicar:	... and will you after each prayer make the response 'Hear us Holy Lord'. Oh God, the Father of all Righteousness, make us a righteous nation.
	(1.5)
Vicar:	Hea⌐r us Holy Lord.
Congregation:	└Hear us Holy Lord.
Vicar:	①→Oh God the Spirit,
	(0.5)
	②→Lord of all Holiness,
	(0.5)
	③→make us a Holy Church
	(0.5)
Congregation:	Hear us Holy Lord.

One reason why three-part lists provide a very suitable and adaptable method for packaging praise or criticism is that listing similar items can work to strengthen, underline or amplify almost any kind of message. This is sometimes done by producing a list which contains three *identical* items, as in extracts (29) and (30) and other familiar examples like 'Well, well, well', 'On and on and on' and 'faster and faster and faster'. One very well-known list of this type from a political speech featured the best-remembered saying of the late Hugh Gaitskell, a former leader of the Labour Party: 'We shall *fight, fight* and *fight* again to save the party we love.' By repeating the word 'fight', he was thus able to make sure that no one could possibly miss it, and at the same time underline the strength of feeling that lay behind the message. A similar effect was also achieved with a three-part list in which each item was repeated by a Conservative cabinet minister, Norman Tebbit, on television during the 1983 general election:

---

(32) (UK general election, 1983)

Tebbit: Labour will spend and spend,
  and borrow and borrow,
  and tax and tax.

More usually, however, three-part lists in political speeches involve more than merely repeating the same words. In extract (33), for example, George Wallace completed a boastful message about his racism by repeating 'segregation', following it each time with a temporal category referring to the present or future. In this way, progressively more emphasis is given to the unchanging firmness of the views for which he had just been elected (arrows pointing up and down indicate rising or falling intonation respectively on the immediately following syllable):

---

(33) (Inaugural speech as governor of Alabama, 1963)

Wallace: ①→... and I say segregation ↑ <u>now</u>
    (0.2)
    ②→segregation to ↑ <u>mor</u>row
    (0.2)
    ③→and segregation for <u>e</u> ↓ ver.
Audience: Hoora– (tape-editor's cut)

In extract (34), Mrs Thatcher used three different categories to conclude a positive assessment of the week's proceedings at a Conservative Party conference, an assertion which is about as literal a boast about 'us' as one could hope to find. By saying that the party is not just united, but is united in three different ways, she is able to expand the scope of the boast while simultaneously amplifying its strength. And the audience in this case starts to respond just before she completes the third item:

```
(34)    (Conservative Party conference, 1980)

Thatcher:       This week has demonstrated (0.4) that we are a
                party united in
            ①→ ↑ purpose
                (0.4)
            ②→strategy
                (0.2)
            ③→and re ↓ sol⌈ve.
Audience:                    ⌊Hear ⌈hear⊢————(8.0)————⊣
Audience:                          ⌊x-xxXXXXXXXXXXXXXxxx-x
```

In these two examples, both speakers display a delicate sense of timing, which is very important if a three-part list is to work as an effective claptrap: delivery of the lists is carefully phased, the items being clearly marked out by similar pauses between each. If an audience anticipates that a three-part list might be under construction, its expectations can then be confirmed at the point where the speaker says 'and' just before the third and final item. However, even when there is no 'and' at all, audiences still tend to treat the completion of a third item as the place to start clapping. In extract (35), for example, they come in immediately after Mr Eric Heffer concludes the third part of a list in the course of delivering a boast about a decision taken by the National Executive Committee of the Labour Party. While he pauses in exactly the same places as Mr Wallace and Mrs Thatcher, he does *not* use 'and' to project the third item as the final one. The audience none the less treats it as such by coming in immediately after he concludes the third part of the list (even though he still had more to say):

61

> **(35) (Fringe meeting, Labour Party conference, 1980)**
>
> *Heffer:* The National Executive decided (0.8) that
> we <u>agreed</u> in <u>PRINCIPLE</u> (0.8) that we
> <u>MUST</u> <u>AGAIN</u> <u>TRY</u> AND <u>GET</u> SOME
> <u>CONSTITUTIONAL AMENDMENTS</u>
> (0.5)
> ①→BE ↑ <u>FORE</u> YOU
> (0.2)
> ②→<u>AT</u> CONFERENCE
> (0.2)
> ③→<u>THIS</u> ↓ <u>WEEK</u>
>
> *Audience:* ⎡SO THAT YOU CAN <u>STILL</u> MAKE⎤
> ⎣xxxXXXXXXXXXXXXXXXXXXXXXXXXXXX⎦=
> *Heffer:* ⎡YOUR <u>MINDS</u> UP
> *Audience:* =⎣XXXXXXXXXXXXXXXX (TV editor's cut)

A common feature of all these examples is that the applaudable messages were technically complete by the time the *first*
item in each list had been delivered. 'I say segregation today',
'we are a party united in purpose' and 'we must again try and
get some constitutional amendments before you' are all gram-
matically complete sentences, and each one is followed by a
pause. Yet there is not so much as a hint of an audience
response at any of these points. This raises the question of how
the audiences knew that there was more to come, and that
applause should therefore be withheld for the time being.

Part of the answer is simply that to have ended the messages
there and then would not have given the audiences enough time
either to recognize that they should respond, or to get ready to
do so. But it is also the case that the speakers all made it quite
clear that 'today', 'purpose' and 'before you' are *not* completion
points, and that they still have more to say. This was done by
delivering these first items in their lists with *rising intonation*
(see upwards-pointing arrows in the transcripts). By contrast,
the termination of an utterance is typically marked by *falling
intonation*, and this is in fact what each of these speakers did on
delivering the last syllable of each of their third and final list
items: 'for e ↓ ver', 're ↓ <u>solve</u>', and 'this ↓ <u>week</u>'. In packaging
applaudable messages, orators are thus able to use intonational

shifts to communicate to the audience whether they are proposing to carry on or come to a close.

Informing the audience that there is more to come is much less of a problem in cases where a list of adjectives or adverbs automatically defers the arrival of a final word, as happened in extract (18). When members of an audience hear Mrs Thatcher start a sentence with the words 'Soviet marxism . . .', they can be confident in treating it as an announcement that some sort of attack or insult is about to be delivered. On this particular occasion, it turns out that there are three things wrong with it, although the precise nature of the criticism does not become apparent until the final word is delivered:

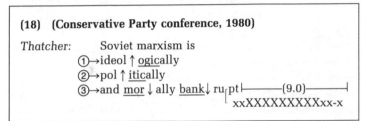

It is noticeable here that Mrs Thatcher does not rely just on the grammatical structure of the sentence to ensure that the audience waits for the arrival of 'bankrupt', but also uses the same intonational shifts as were seen in the other examples: the first two items in the list are each concluded with rising intonation, and the third with a fall on the last beat.

The general importance of intonation and associated variations in volume and rhythmic stress is underlined by the fact that it is sometimes possible to anticipate where an audience will applaud in the course of speeches made in languages we do not understand. The process of recognition is also greatly assisted by the way speakers produce their talk in conjunction with a variety of precisely timed non-verbal activities. By combining these different techniques to package and deliver their messages, orators can communicate to their audiences that a change of mood or tempo is taking place. They can signal that they are, as it were, 'changing gear', and launching into a sequence which will be worthy of closer attention and perhaps even applause. The most obvious case of this in the examples seen so far is the excerpt from Mr Heffer's fringe-meeting speech at the 1980 Labour Party conference.

---

(35) (Fringe meeting, Labour Party conference, 1980)

Heffer: The National Executive decided (0.8) that
we agreed in PRINCIPLE (0.8) that we MUST
AGAIN TRY AND GET SOME CONSTITUTION-
AL AMENDMENTS (0.5) BE ↑ FORE YOU (0.2)
AT   CONFERENCE   (0.2)   THIS   ↓ WEEK
⌐SO THAT YOU CAN STILL MAKE YOUR
⌐xxx XXXXXXXXXXXXXXXXXXXXXXXXXXXXXX
⌐MINDS UP

Audience: XXXXXX

(*indicates the lowest point reached by the hand in a downward-pointing gesture)

At the exact point where the first 'we' signals the start of the applaudable message, Mr Heffer produces the first in a series of sharp downward-pointing gestures with his right hand. He raises his voice, first at 'principle' and then again at 'must', after which he continues to shout out the rest of his message at the same volume. More pointing gestures follow, each one being timed to coincide precisely with stressed vowel sounds. This gives the general impression that he is beating out the rhythm of the words with a view to making absolutely sure that his point is well and truly driven home. When it comes to producing the three-part list, each stage in its delivery is clearly marked out by the use of a progressively longer stabbing gesture. His arm finally reaches its maximum point of extension in the middle of the third item, and his hand then changes direction and sweeps sideways across the front of his body (see plate 3.2)

From quite an early stage in this sequence, the audience is positively bombarded with a variety of different signals, all of which point in the same direction: 'this week' is projected as the place for an audience response by the fact that it comes at the end of an applaudable message which began with a noticeable increase in volume, gestural activity and rhythmic emphasis. It is also the third item in a list, and is marked as the final one both

3.2 Mr Heffer's gestures become progressively more expansive with each item in a list of three (extract 35).

'... before you ...'

'... at conference ...'

'... this week ...'

by falling intonation on the last beat, and by the most sweeping stabbing gesture so far. The techniques deployed by Mr Heffer were thus so numerous and unmistakable that it is hardly surprising that the audience responded so promptly.

One reason why Mr Heffer was able to deploy such expansive gestures is that he was not speaking from a written text. By contrast, speakers who rely on scripts are much more restricted when it comes to using non-verbal signals. This is because gestures look very unnatural when not co-ordinated with talk that is spontaneous or 'off the cuff'. From the speaker's point of view, it is extremely difficult in sheer practical terms to produce flamboyant movements of the hands and arms at the same time as referring to a script. If he looks up from his text and then produces such a gesture, it is almost certain to appear badly timed, and might even arouse suspicions among the audience that the gestures themselves had actually been written into the script. The speaker who strays too far from his text also runs a serious risk of losing his place. This can be an embarrassing enough experience in itself, but is even worse if the speaker finds himself stranded in the middle of a series of gestures without being able to remember what to say next.

The importance of being seen to be able to speak confidently without continually referring to a text is such that some politicians have made a practice of learning their scripts by heart before giving speeches. More recently, technology has come to their aid by making it possible for them to read their scripts from transparent teleprompter screens. The words, which are transmitted from a back room on to flat perspex screens, can be clearly seen by the speaker, but are invisible to the audience. Speaking with the aid of this technology, politicians can appear to be continually addressing their audience, as they move their heads from side to side (i.e. screen to screen) and look 'through' the screens. Interestingly, it has been dubbed the 'sincerity machine', and was first used in Britain by President Reagan in his speech to members of parliament at Westminster in 1982 (see plate 3.3). The only British politician to have used it extensively is Mrs Thatcher who relied heavily on it during the 1983 general election.

Previously, Mrs Thatcher was a very 'script-bound' orator, and was unable to make much use of expressive non-verbal actions. However, this is not to say that script-bound speakers

Words on screens
can be read by
speaker but are
invisible to audience

TV sets in boxes
reflect script
on to screens above

3.3 Ronald Reagan using the 'sincerity machine' to deliver his speech at Westminster in 1982. The words on the transparent screens (arrowed) can only be seen by the speaker and are invisible to the audience. They are reflected on to the screens from TV sets facing upwards from the floor (concealed in arrowed boxes). Behind the scenes, an assistant winds the script in front of a TV camera which relays it into the hall.

3.4 Mrs Thatcher goes for applause with a three-parted boast about party unity (extract 34).

'... united in ...'

'... purpose ...'

'... strategy ...'

'... and re- ...'

'... solve.'

(Closes mouth and clears throat.)

are prevented from using any non-verbal signals at all, as can be clearly seen by looking a little more closely at the way Mrs Thatcher speaks when reading her text from papers on a lectern rather than from transparent teleprompter screens.

Like most speakers who seldom stray from their prepared scripts, Mrs Thatcher continually moves her head up and down from lectern to audience and back again. When video tapes of her speaking are played at faster speed than normal, it emerges that the timing and direction of her glances are remarkably rhythmic, and go through a cycle of movements that keep recurring at very regular intervals and in much the same order. After looking up from her script, she hardly ever looks straight ahead at the audience, but directs her gaze at those to her left or right. The usual pattern involves about three glances to the left followed by one to the right, and the sheer regularity of these movements may be one of the factors which has contributed to the view held in some quarters that her public-speaking style has a tendency to be rather monotonous.

A hint as to what typically happens when she is going for applause has already been given in the second frame of plate 3.1, where her head started to move down to the text as she started to say the first syllable of 'Whitelaw'. In fact, this retreat to the lectern after a glance to her left occurs extremely regularly during her last one or two syllables prior to an audience response. But because the picture switched to Mr Whitelaw before she had finished saying his name, and before her head had reached its destination, it was in that case impossible to see two other things that regularly happen immediately after she reaches such completion points. They are, however, visible on the video tapes of extracts (18) and (34), and are illustrated in plate 3.4.

These show that, after bringing her head down from the left, Mrs Thatcher visibly closes her mouth, and then promptly clears her throat. As these things are usually done after the first few claps have already started, they appear to be retrospective signals, or confirmations, that the time has indeed come for the audience to show their approval: by closing her mouth so noticeably she indicates that she has finished for the time being, and by clearing her throat she shows that she is putting the few seconds break to good use in getting herself ready to carry on once the applause is over. Anyone in the audience who has still failed to notice that it is time to applaud is therefore provided with two final reminders as to what should now be done.

It might seem that a slight head movement of this sort is too subtle a signal to play any significant part in the delivery of a successful claptrap. But there are at least two reasons for thinking otherwise. One is the sheer regularity with which the [head-down] [mouth-close] [throat-clear] sequence occurs at completion points that precede bursts of applause during Mrs Thatcher's speeches. The other emerges from a case where things nearly went badly wrong as she was producing a boast about her government's achievements. As can be seen from extract (36), the audience, or rather a small portion of it, produced a brief flutter of applause just after the third item in a list, but withdrew when it turned out that she had quite a lot more to say:

---

(36)   (Conservative Party conference, 1980)

Thatcher: As you know we've made the first crucial
          changes in trade union law
               (0.4)
     ①→to remove the worst abuses of the closed shop
               (0.2)
     ②→to restrict picketing to the place of work of the
          parties in dis ↑ <u>pute</u>
               (0.2)
     ③→and   to   encourage   secret   <u>bal</u> ↓ lots
               ⌜hhhh Jim Prior has carried <u>all</u> these⌝=
Audience: ⌞x-xx-xxxxxxxxxxxxxxxxxxxxxxxxxxxx-xx-x-⌟

Thatcher: = measures   through   with   the   support
          of   the   vast   majority   of   trade   union
          memb⌜ers ⊢————(10.0)————⊣
Audience: ⌞x-xxXXXXXXXXXXXXXXxx-x

What happens in this case is that the devices used by Mrs Thatcher point in quite opposite directions, some indicating that 'ballots' is the completion point, and others that she will continue beyond that. Those who produced the flutter of applause were presumably responding to the fact that 'to encourage secret ballots' was the third item in a list which completes the boast about changes in trade union law, that it was projected as the last item by a preceding 'and', and was delivered with falling intonation on the final beat. On the other hand, Mrs Thatcher's head came up from the lectern during 'ballots', and she took a huge and highly visible breath of air immediately afterwards (shown by 'hhhh' in the transcript). Both these moves signal an intention to carry on talking rather than to stop and let the audience applaud.

The confusion which occurs in the middle of the sequence thus appears to arise because Mrs Thatcher uses techniques which convey conflicting messages to the audience. A minority responds to those which project 'ballots' as the completion point, while the majority responds to her moving her head upwards and taking in a breath of air. The longer-than-usual burst of applause that eventually follows may partly reflect a concern on the part of the audience to compensate for the earlier error. It might also be responsive to the fact that Mrs Thatcher had by then completed *two* different types of applaudable message: a boast about 'us' and a commendation of Mr Prior.

More generally, the sequence is of special interest because it provides strong support for the earlier suggestion that the packaging and delivery of a successful claptrap require the use of several techniques at the same time, all of which should point in the *same* direction. It shows how difficulties can arise when this is not done, and when some signals point towards completion and some towards continuation. It also shows that a speaker can communicate a great deal by using brief non-verbal signals such as breathing in and glancing up at the audience.

Since starting to use the 'sincerity machine', Mrs Thatcher has slightly increased her use of other non-verbal actions. As she moves towards an applaudable completion point, she now tends to raise her forearm repeatedly, and emphasize the stressed vowel sounds of her words with her left hand half-clenched. The [mouth-close] [throat-clear] parts of the former pattern remain, but she seems to exhibit a degree of uncertainty as to whether or not and where to move her head during the last syllable or two. Given the observations about the importance of mobilizing several devices at once, it is of some interest that preliminary work on her new teleprompter-aided speaking style suggests that silences (averaging about half a second) between completion points and the start of applause during her speeches, are now much more frequent than is the case when she has a script on a lectern. Delayed audience responses of this kind also tend to feature in speeches by Ronald Reagan. From the point of view of assuring a prompt response from the audience being addressed, there may therefore be disadvantages in using a sincerity machine. However, as will be seen later, this may not matter at all when it comes to impressing the much larger audiences who see such excerpts on television.

As for three-part lists, they are by no means the most common type of verbal format used in applause-elicitation sequences, and present estimates suggest that they probably feature in no more than 15 per cent of cases. A much more frequently used verbal format, which may be employed in as many as one in three of all sequences where applause occurs during political speeches, packages applaudable messages as a two-part contrast or antithesis.

Contrastive pairs

As so much political debate involves assertions and counter-assertions about 'us' and 'them', it is hardly surprising that making a contrast between two items is an extraordinarily adaptable and widely used technique for packaging and delivering applaudable messages. It is also one which was well known to the classical Greek and Roman writers on oratory who described a variety of different types of antitheses in their classifications of 'rhetorical figures'.

Contrasts work in such a way as to have considerable advantages both for projecting a completion point and for delivering a punch line that is likely to appeal to an audience in a way that is similar to that of the punch line of a good joke. If the speaker can present his audience with some sort of puzzle, he stands a good chance of arousing their curiosity, and thus giving them more of an incentive to pay attention. They will then be in a good position to recognize and appreciate whatever solution is provided by the punch line. This is what happens in extract (20), where Liberal Party leader David Steel begins by claiming that there are two Conservative parties in the election. After posing this puzzle, he pauses before proceeding to offer a solution in two distinct phases. This involves making a contrast between the policies of the Conservative and Labour parties, and doing so in a way that is insulting to both of them:

(20)   (UK general election, 1979)

Steel: THE TRUTH <u>IS</u> BEGINNING TO <u>DAW</u>N ON
                    OUR <u>PEOPLE</u> THAT THERE ARE ↑<u>TWO</u>
                    CONSERVATIVE   <u>PARTIES</u>   ↓IN   THIS
                    ↓ELECTION
                       (0.6)

      Ⓐ→ ⎰ <u>ONE</u> IS OFFERING THE CONTINUATION
           ⎱ OF THE POLICIES WE'VE HAD FOR THE
              LAST FIVE ↑YEARS
                       (0.2)

      Ⓑ→ ⎰ AND THE OTHER IS OFFERING A RE↓TURN
           ⎱ TO THE ↓POLICIES ↓OF <u>FORTY</u> YEARS
              A⌈↓GO

Audience: ⌊Heh h⌈eh heh
Audience: ⌊xXXXXXXXXXXXXXXX ....

It can be seen that the intonational shifts used here are very
similar to those featured in the delivery of three-part lists. At the
end of the first part of the contrast, rising intonation on 'years'
signals that there is more to come, while the continuously
falling contour throughout the second part indicates that the
message is approaching completion. The fact that the second
part will be the last part is also communicated by the use of
'and'. Other details which are typical of the way contrasts are
produced are the similarities in length, content and grammatical structure of the two parts. The second half is thus a slightly
modified mirror image of the first, the only changes made the
second time around being ones which involve the direct
substitution of words and phrases that clearly contrast with
those used in the first part: 'one' becomes 'the other', 'the
continuation of' becomes 'a return to' and 'the last five years'
becomes 'forty years ago'. Once members of the audience have
recognized that a contrast is being delivered, it is easy enough
for them to anticipate exactly when the completion point will
be reached. In this particular case, the first part of the contrast
ended with reference to a period of time after the word
'policies', so it is reasonable to expect that the applaudable
message will be concluded when 'policies' is again followed by
a similar temporal reference in the second sentence.

74

In a very similar example, Mrs Thatcher uses a rhetorical question to pose a puzzle, which is again resolved by the two parts of a contrast:

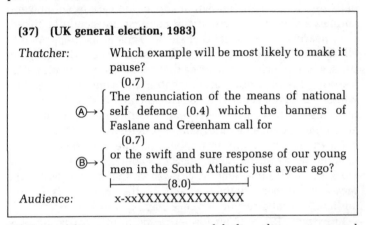

(37)   (UK general election, 1983)

Thatcher: Which example will be most likely to make it pause?
    (0.7)
Ⓐ→ { The renunciation of the means of national self defence (0.4) which the banners of Faslane and Greenham call for
    (0.7)
Ⓑ→ { or the swift and sure response of our young men in the South Atlantic just a year ago?
    ├————(8.0)————┤
Audience: x-xxXXXXXXXXXXXXX

While puzzles are sometimes posed before the contrast and resolved when both parts have been completed, they are also often posed in the first part and resolved by the second part. In extract (38), for example, Mr Callaghan presents his audience with the puzzle of why he is not planning to do what most party leaders usually do during election campaigns, and answers it by contrasting his own intentions favourably with the disreputable tactics referred to in the first part:

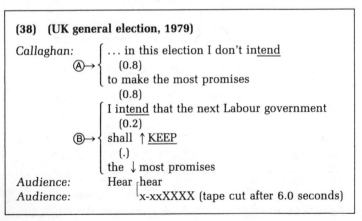

(38)   (UK general election, 1979)

Callaghan: Ⓐ→ { ... in this election I don't in<u>tend</u>
    (0.8)
    to make the most promises
    (0.8)
    Ⓑ→ { I in<u>tend</u> that the next Labour government
    (0.2)
    shall ↑<u>KEEP</u>
    (.)
    the ↓most promises
Audience: Hear ⌈hear
Audience: ⌊x-xxXXXX (tape cut after 6.0 seconds)

75

Here, the main change is from 'make the most promises' to 'keep the most promises', and it is noticeable that the word which carries the key to the contrast and the answer to the puzzle is delivered with rising intonation and an increase in volume and emphasis. The two parts of the contrast are carefully timed, with nearly a whole second of silence separating them. As if to allow time for the message to sink in after 'keep', Mr Callaghan pauses briefly before indicating that completion is imminent by lowering his intonation and repeating the same phrase as that which has been used earlier to bring the first part of the contrast to a close. It was seen earlier that repeating the name of a film after announcing an award-winner provided the audience with extra time to get ready to applaud on cue, and repeating the concluding words of the first part of a contrast would appear to work in exactly the same way. By then, the crucial part of the message has been delivered, and all that remains is for the audience to get a response under way.

In extract (19), another former prime minister used more or less identical techniques to those deployed by Mr Callaghan in the above example.

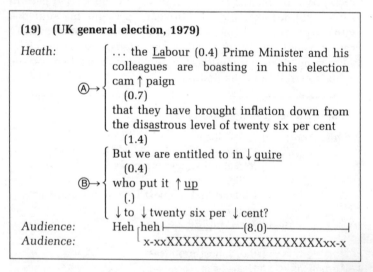

(19)   (UK general election, 1979)

Heath: ... the Labour (0.4) Prime Minister and his
                colleagues are boasting in this election
      Ⓐ→   cam ↑ paign
                    (0.7)
                that they have brought inflation down from
                the disastrous level of twenty six per cent
                    (1.4)
                But we are entitled to in ↓ quire
                    (0.4)
      Ⓑ→   who put it ↑ up
                    (.)
                ↓ to ↓ twenty six per ↓ cent?
Audience: Heh ┌heh├──────────(8.0)──────────┤
Audience: └x-xxXXXXXXXXXXXXXXXXXXXXXxx-x

In the timing of his delivery, the added stress and rising intonation on the key contrastive word 'up', the slight pause after it and the subsequent falling intonation as the concluding phrase from the first part is repeated, Mr Heath produces an almost exact replica of the Callaghan sequence in extract (38).

The importance of producing two contrasting parts which closely resemble each other in length and content can be most clearly seen by looking at cases which misfire. One such example has already been seen in extract (7), where former Labour cabinet minister Peter Shore's audience delayed for a whole second before responding with only five seconds of rather hesitant and feeble applause. This is one of a number of instances in which trouble arises after an extremely lengthy second part of a contrast:

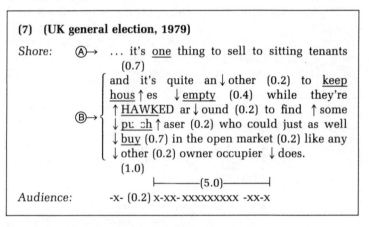

(7) (UK general election, 1979)

Shore: Ⓐ→   ... it's one thing to sell to sitting tenants
                    (0.7)
          Ⓑ→   ⌠ and it's quite an ↓other (0.2) to keep
                    hous ↑ es ↓ empty (0.4) while they're
                    ↑ HAWKED ar ↓ ound (0.2) to find ↑ some
                    ↓ pu ch ↑ aser (0.2) who could just as well
                    ↓ buy (0.7) in the open market (0.2) like any
                    ⌊ ↓ other (0.2) owner occupier ↓ does.
                    (1.0)
                    ├———(5.0)———┤
Audience: -x- (0.2) x-xx- xxxxxxxxx -xx-x

Not only is the second part of the contrast long and drawn out, but it also fails to echo the words and phrases used in the first. What appears to happen as a result of this is that the audience loses the thread, the connections between the two parts being obscured as Mr Shore goes on and on producing one more staccato burst of talk after another. If the earlier and more successful extracts are anything to go by, Mr Shore might have had more luck if he had said something in which the second part of the contrast more closely mirrored the first. Using the Callaghan and Heath examples as a model, something like the following would almost certainly have stood a better chance of success.

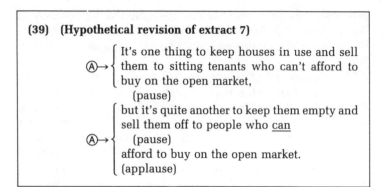

(39)   (Hypothetical revision of extract 7)

(A)→ It's one thing to keep houses in use and sell them to sitting tenants who can't afford to buy on the open market,
        (pause)
(A)→ but it's quite another to keep them empty and sell them off to people who <u>can</u>
        (pause)
     afford to buy on the open market.
     (applause)

A similarly poorly balanced contrastive pair was produced by Mr Heath in extract (40), but unlike Mr Shore he did not wait around for the audience to get the message and start clapping. He proceeded to refer back to and summarize the gist of the point he had just made (arrowed in the transcript), whereupon the audience came in with a perfectly respectable burst of applause:

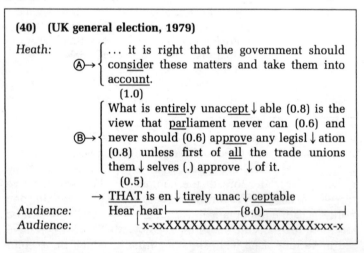

(40)   (UK general election, 1979)

Heath:
(A)→ ... it is right that the government should con<u>sid</u>er these matters and take them into ac<u>count</u>.
        (1.0)
(B)→ What is enti<u>re</u>ly unac<u>cept</u> ↓ able (0.8) is the view that <u>par</u>liament never can (0.6) and never should (0.6) ap<u>prove</u> any legisl ↓ ation (0.8) unless first of <u>all</u> the trade unions them ↓ selves (.) approve ↓ of it.
        (0.5)
→ <u>THAT</u> is en ↓ <u>tire</u>ly unac ↓ <u>cept</u>able

Audience: Hear ⌜hear⊢————————(8.0)————————⊣
Audience: ⌞x-xxXXXXXXXXXXXXXXXXXXXXXXxxx-x

Going in pursuit of applause, as Mr Heath does in this case, is quite a common response of speakers who find themselves faced with a deathly silence after the completion of a claptrap. A very usual way of doing this is to refer back to what they have just said, and to summarize the gist of the applaudable message. By recompleting it, speakers effectively tell the audience that the point deserves more attention than it has so far received, and that continuing to make another one is less important than mentioning the previous one again. The audience is therefore put under considerable pressure to provide a concrete demonstration that the message has been received, understood *and* appreciated.

The same type of pursuit strategy is also used by former Liberal MP John Pardoe in extract (41), which illustrates another kind of error that can cause a claptrap to misfire. The problem with this is not that the contrast suffers from long-windedness, but that it is far too brief and is delivered too close to the final completion point. As a result, the audience hardly has enough time to realize what has happened, let alone to get a response under way:

---

(41) (UK general election, 1979)

Pardoe: ... and which will <u>GUARANTEE</u> (0.5) what is
perhaps the <u>most</u> important thing that <u>can</u> be
↓ guaran ↓ teed,
  (1.0)
that ↑ NO ONE IN ↓ BRITAIN CAN
↓ EVER A ↓ GAIN BE BETTER OFF
Ⓐ→BY ↓ <u>NOT</u> WORKING
Ⓑ→THAN ↓ WORKING.
  (0.8)
THAT'S THE ↑ <u>FIRST</u> ↓ thing to guaran ↓ tee.
├————————(5.0)————————┤

Audience: -x-xx-xxxxxxxxxxxxxxx-xx-x-x

In this case, what the contrast amounts to does not become clear until the very last word in the sentence. As a result, there is no space after that for the audience to get ready to applaud. Also, the two parts of the contrast are not clearly marked out as such with an intervening pause as is usual in more successful cases. The crucial importance of careful timing in the build-up to a completion point is thus further highlighted by this example. It also shows that raising one's voice and delivering what follows with falling intonation are not powerful enough to work on their own as a means of eliciting a response, however clearly they may signal that the speaker has just launched into such a sequence.

These last two examples show that all is not necessarily lost when silence threatens, and that speakers can use pursuit devices to prod a reluctant audience into responding. In fact, such devices work so well that they can almost be said to possess a 'can't lose' character: not only are they reliable methods for eliciting applause when none has yet started, but if they are used *after* it has already got under way, the speaker then gains the advantage of being seen to be applauded much earlier than would otherwise have been the case. An example of this is extract (42), where former Labour Party leader Michael Foot went on to say 'That's what we're here for' after the crowd had already started to respond just before the end of a contrast:

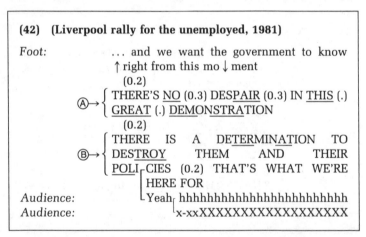

In the earlier excerpt from a speech by Mr Eric Heffer (extract 35), it was seen that speakers sometimes mark out the items in a list with differentiated non-verbal actions. Similar gestural partitioning also often features in the delivery of contrasts, a point that can be illustrated with reference to the way Mr Foot uses hand movements in extract (42). As he begins the first part of the contrast, he raises his right hand to a position where it is level with his head, with the palm facing outwards towards the crowd. On each of the stressed beats in 'THERE'S <u>NO</u> (0.3) DES<u>PAIR</u> (0.3) IN <u>THIS</u> (.) <u>GREAT</u> (.) <u>DEMONSTRA</u>TION', he pats the air, moving the hand forward about 9 inches each time. Then, as he embarks on the second part of the contrast, he holds it still in the upright position without moving it at all until he gets to the first syllable of '<u>POLIC</u>IES', the last word in the contrast. At that point, he moves it sharply forwards and downwards as far as it will go. As can be seen from the transcript, the first response of the crowd comes in *immediately* after that. The two parts of the contrast are thus clearly distinguished and partitioned by the use of different accompanying gestures, and the arrival of the completion point is heralded by a sudden swoop of the hand on the stressed first syllable of the final word. So soon after this gesture does the crowd response start that the sequence is strongly reminiscent of the way an orchestra comes in at the wave of the conductor's baton (see plate 3.5)

In other ways too, this excerpt is an exemplary case of how to use a contrast to maximum effect. Thus, Mr Foot begins by telling the crowd that he is about to say something that is addressed to the government on 'our' behalf, or in other words that an applaudable message is on the way. Having alerted them to this, he produces the first part of a contrast which is both a boast about the morale of 'us' demonstrators, and something of a puzzle, the question to be answered being that of why there is no despair among a crowd of several thousand unemployed people. After a slight pause, the second part of the contrast supplies a solution in the form of a double-edged punch line, which continues the boast about 'our' morale ('determination') in building an attack on 'them' ('... to destroy them and their policies'). In addition to the carefully timed delivery and gestural partitioning of the two parts of the contrast, the sequence also has 'poetic' qualities, alliteration and rhyme being involved in 'despair', 'demonstration', 'determination', 'destroy'.

A variety of verbal and non-verbal techniques are thus combined and co-ordinated in building up a highly successful claptrap, which subsequently gains in effect by the tagging on of a recompleting assertion after it has already become unnecessary for the speaker to go in pursuit of applause. Not only does

3.5 Mr Foot marks out the two parts of a contrast and rounds it off with a downward thrust of his arm (extract 42).

'... There's no despair in ...'

'... this great demonstration ...'

this ensure that the response is then seen to be an extremely early one, but the fact that the pursuit is drowned by the clapping and cheering makes the reception look and sound an exceptionally enthusiastic one. This view of the excerpt, together with the opinion that it is an example of technically skilled oratory in action, was apparently shared by at least one group of people with a vested interest in political persuasion. This particular extract from Mr Foot's speech was thus selected and used as the concluding sequence of a televised party political broadcast on behalf of the Labour Party, which ended with the slogan 'If you want to defeat unemployment in Britain, join us' being screened and read aloud over film of the applauding crowd.

'... there is a
determination to
destroy
them and their ...'
(holds hand
motionless)

'... policies ...' (hand
swoops downwards off
screen)

Generality and simplicity

Just as most cases of audiences applauding politicians occur
only after commendations, boasts and insults, so too are there
only a limited number of ways in which such messages can be
effectively packaged and delivered. At the beginning of this
chapter we saw that the dictionary definition of 'claptrap' is 'a
trick, device, or language designed to catch applause'. Close
observation of how politicians talk just prior to favourable
audience responses reveals that the secret of successful claptrap
production lies in the simultaneous and co-ordinated use of
relatively few verbal and non-verbal techniques which signal to
audiences *that* they should start clapping and *when* they should

do so. Generally speaking, the more devices a speaker deploys, the better are his chances of receiving an immediate response of adequate duration and intensity. The skilful orator can thus lead his audience step by step towards the point where clapping should start as surely as if he had shouted 'Hip, hip – Hooray!' or 'On your marks, get set – Go!'

Of the various techniques available to politicians, the verbal formats described here appear to be among those most regularly used in applause-elicitation sequences. There are a number of others which work in a similar way, and more detailed studies of these are currently in progress.

The findings reported so far support a view of what is involved when audiences applaud politicians that flies in the face of more conventional beliefs about the 'spontaneous' or 'voluntary' character of such displays of approval. They suggest that favourable audience responses are almost always prompted by the politicians themselves. If they are to be sure of obtaining an immediate response of adequate duration and intensity, *how they speak* can be seen to matter at least as much as *what they actually say*. Even apparently small errors in the packaging, timing and delivery of messages can easily confuse the audience both as to whether or not and when they should start to applaud. Moreover, these conclusions stand irrespective of the particular political party or beliefs a speaker happens to represent, with the same types of message and the same packaging techniques apparently working equally well for *all* politicians.

One question arising from all this is how far it applies to political speeches made in languages other than English. An adequate answer to this will obviously have to await the results of further research, but there is already preliminary evidence suggesting that applause-elicitation sequences work in much the same way in France, Germany and the Netherlands. From further afield, some intriguing observations about the situation in Iran since the Islamic revolution have recently come to hand. Clapping has evidently been banned as a decadent western practice, and has been replaced by the chanting of slogans like 'Death to the imperialists!' Recordings of speeches by the Ayatollah Khomeini reveal not just that such chants regularly occur in response to three-part lists and contrasts, but that they tend to last for between *six* and *eight* seconds. The fact that the average duration is slightly shorter than that for applause is, of course, perfectly consistent with the earlier observation that vocal responses can be got under way more quickly than ones relying on moving the hands (see chapter 2). More generally, the preliminary evidence from these other countries suggests that the findings reported here may eventually be shown to have cross-cultural applicability far beyond the English-speaking world.

A question sometimes asked about these findings is whether the business of applause elicitation can really be as simple as this. The most likely answer to this is not just that it is indeed this simple, but that it may very well *have to be* this simple because of the sheer size of the audiences national politicians address. As we noted in chapter 1, the problem of securing and holding the attention of an audience becomes more and more difficult as the size of a group increases. An increase in numbers also progressively restricts the complexity of the ideas it is possible to put across, as well as the linguistic forms that can be used to convey them. As any teacher or lecturer knows, the content and style of his teaching are greatly affected by the size of his classes. With a small group, it is possible to discuss and explain highly technical matters, whereas in a large lecture theatre it is very difficult to do more than provide simplified outlines of more complex bodies of knowledge. The techniques used by politicians may thus seem to be excessively simple and obvious, but it is important to remember that there may be no other practicable options open to speakers faced with the problem of communicating with a large number of people at once.

Just as some teachers are more effective than others, so too are some orators better able to impress audiences than their competitors. This raises the further question of what it is about the way some politicians make a speech that gains them recognition as outstanding orators. If there are only a limited number of techniques available for attracting audience approval, just what does it mean to be a technically accomplished speaker? And if a purely observational approach makes it possible to discover how the most regularly used techniques work, can it also help us to understand how spellbinding oratory works, and why a minority of politicians come to be regarded as 'charismatic' leaders?

4 Charisma

Tony Benn: a case study in spellbinding oratory

After the defeat of the Labour Party at the 1979 general election, Mr Tony Benn became a much more visible public figure than he had been as a cabinet minister in the Wilson and Callaghan governments. He rapidly emerged as the leading spokesman for the 'hard left' of the party, an achievement which depended heavily on his exceptional skill as an orator. His speaking engagements regularly attract large audiences, and press reports frequently comment on the rapturous receptions he typically receives. He also makes a very large number of speeches, subjecting himself to a punishing schedule with which few other contemporary politicians can compete. For example, it was estimated that he made over 400 speeches during 1980 (not counting those made on the floor of the House of Commons). He therefore not only averaged more than one speech a day, but his overall total for the year was greater than that achieved in an entire lifetime by some of the most famous orators of classical Greece.

Over the past few years, the major part of Mr Benn's speaking programme has been directed to the grassroots of the Labour Party, and there is little doubt that this has had an important impact both on his own career and on the recent history of his party. Although he was narrowly defeated by Mr Denis Healey in the 1981 election for the deputy leadership of the Labour Party, he took *80 per cent* of the local constituency parties' votes within the electoral college. In the aftermath, his relations with the leadership of the party became increasingly strained and distant. But by early 1983, a leader article in *The Times* acknowledged his enduring effectiveness as a speaker by asking whether the Labour Party could really afford to go into the next general election without its most impressive orator as part of its front-bench team. In the event, he remained in the wings, but Bennite policies none the less played an important part in the 1983 campaign. The composition of the constituency Mr Benn had represented for thirty years had been radically altered by boundary changes, and Mr Benn lost his seat in the House of Commons. In 1984, however, he fought and won a by-election, becoming MP for Chesterfield.

While the media and the electorate are willing and able to recognize an outstanding public speaker when they hear one, they seldom stop to ask exactly what it is that enables them to do so. Mr Benn's opponents like to dismiss him as a 'demagogue' or 'rabble-rouser', while his supporters stress that his impact derives from the popularity of his policies, rather than any particular personal skills or attributes. However, neither of these explanations will really do. Even if he is able to rouse an audience, the fact is that most politicians are incapable of rallying their supporters anything like as effectively as he can. On the other hand, the suggestion that his impact derives solely from his policies ignores the fact that he is just one among a number of professional politicians who subscribe to them, and thus fails to deal with the question of why he, rather than someone else, became the leading spokesman for the hard left.

The weakness of conventional explanations of why one orator is more effective than another lies in the fact that people find it very difficult to take a dispassionate view of politicians. Opponents may fear that to recognize technical excellence in one of their enemies will be mistaken as paying him a compliment, while supporters tend not to like the idea that the impact of their hero may be merely a result of technical skill. In trying to discover how effective oratory works, then, the main challenge is to leave one's political preferences on one side as a preliminary to looking closely at how such politicians actually make the speeches through which they achieve recognition as spellbinding orators. By concentrating on the output of someone like Mr Benn, it is thus possible to subject his techniques to detailed scrutiny, and to compare them with those used both by more run-of-the-mill speakers, and by others with similarly outstanding reputations. When this is done, it becomes clear that there are a number of technical skills which may be common to all great orators.

Freedom of expression

A first and most obvious point about Mr Benn's speaking style is that, in common with most great orators, he is hardly ever to be seen using a script. It was noted in the previous chapter that script-bound speakers are much more restricted in the use they can make of gestures, and that this is one reason why they are likely to appear less spontaneous than politicians who are able to speak 'off the cuff'. The greater freedom to add emphasis with carefully co-ordinated movements of the arms, hands, head or body is also important when it comes to communicating with very large audiences. In particular, they make it easier for those at the back of a hall to follow what the speaker is saying: even if they cannot hear very well, they are at least able to see that the speaker is alive and is putting some effort into the delivery of his speech.

Freedom from a text also enables speakers to sustain more continuous eye contact with an audience and, as was noted in chapter 1, keeping those being addressed under constant surveillance is one way of holding their attention. In fact, humans are the only primate species in which the irises are framed by visible areas of whiteness, and it is generally considered that the evolutionary significance of this has to do with the communicative importance of our eyes: the whites of the eyes make it relatively easy for people to track even slight movements over quite large distances. An illustration of the

4.1 Carefully co-ordinated gestures can be important for communicating with large audiences. Tony Benn frequently puts both hands to work in getting his points across.

4.2 Prominent eyes, like those of Tony Benn (top left), are more likely to be visible from the back row, while those of spectacle-wearers like Denis Healey (below left) may be obscured from view, even at very close range. Mr Benn's habit of removing his glasses before making a speech (right) is thus a sensible pre-caution to take.

importance of eye visibility for holding the attention of an audience is provided by an anecdote in the autobiography of the Oxford philosopher, A. J. Ayer (*Part of My Life*, 1977). He reports that, after sustaining a black eye as a result of bumping into a lamp post during a wartime blackout, he took to wearing dark glasses. He goes on to say that he subsequently found when lecturing in them that it was quite impossible to hold the attention of an audience. Given his reputation as an effective speaker, this suggests that the invisibility of a person's eyes can seriously interfere with his ability to communicate with an audience. It may therefore be no coincidence that there have been very few great orators who have worn spectacles, even with plain glass in them, while making speeches. And some,

like Hitler, went to great lengths never to be seen or photo-graphed in public while wearing glasses.

As far as Mr Benn is concerned, it is interesting to note that his more vindictive critics sometimes claim that he has 'mad staring eyes', a point he has occasionally even joked about in some of his own speeches. In fact, his eyes are rather large, and this may actually be a much more important communicative asset than he or his critics realize. It presumably means that more people will be able to track more of his eye movements over a greater distance than is possible in the case of speakers with less prominent eyes. The rate at which Mr Benn blinks his eyes while making a speech is also much lower than is the case with most other orators, and this may further contribute to the visibility of his eyes. At the same time, however, it is a detail which has probably contributed to his gaze being described as 'staring'.

Being free to spend more time looking at the audience than is possible when tied to a text provides a speaker with another useful practical advantage. It means that he is in a much better position to monitor and respond to the reactions of his listeners to what he is saying. If he sees signs of puzzlement, he can take immediate steps to clarify or elaborate on the point he is trying to get across. If he sees signs of boredom, he can do something to liven things up. And if he sees signs of approval, he may be able to capitalize on them in what he says next. By contrast, the script-bound orator is less likely to have such a good appreciation of how the audience is reacting, and will therefore find it much more difficult to depart from his text and improvise in as responsive a fashion as ex tempore speakers like Mr Benn.

There are also other ways in which speakers who stick closely to a script are likely to sound less than fully spontaneous, passionate, impressive or sympathetic to the audience being addressed. By reading out a speech, a politician makes it quite clear that it was carefully prepared beforehand, that it would have been delivered to any audience that happened to be there at the time, and that it will be ploughed through from start to finish and without regard for whether or not it holds the attention of this particular audience. The well-known fact that professional politicians often employ speech-writers also means that the use of a prepared script may raise doubts about the authorship of the speech. And to be suspected of merely mouthing someone else's words is certainly not the surest way of impressing an audience.

The disadvantages associated with being seen to read from a script no doubt explain why some of the most effective orators will go to great lengths to avoid having to do so. Some, like the late Iain Macleod, who was once tipped as a future Conservative Party leader, would spend a great deal of time writing out speeches and learning them off by heart prior to delivery. Similarly, the late Aneurin Bevan, who is widely regarded as one of the greatest post-war British orators, would sometimes take the trouble to anticipate the sorts of interruption likely to come from hecklers on the Tory side of the House of Commons, and work out suitable responses beforehand. When things went according to plan, he was thus able to counter-attack with what looked like an impressive display of spontaneous and quick-witted repartee. More recently, Ronald Reagan and Margaret Thatcher have used new technology in the quest for spontaneity. At least since his speech in 1980 accepting the Republican nomination as presidential candidate, Mr Reagan has made use of the 'sincerity machine' (described in chapter 3), and his success in appearing to speak spontaneously was underlined in a *Time* magazine article which described the immense amount of work that went into preparing the acceptance speech. This was not, however, evident from the way he delivered it:

the entire speech sounded as though it was delivered off the top of Reagan's head, that the thoughts had just occurred to him and, darn it, he was going to share them with his friends all over America. Said Wisconsin's Republican Governor Lee Dreyfus, a Ph.D. in communications: 'I'd give him an A if he were in my class.' That was the mark generally awarded Reagan.... Iowa's G.O.P. Governor Robert Ray, who has been cool to Reagan in the past, called the address 'dynamite. He touched the soul of America. He's off to a flying start.' (*Time*, 28 July 1980, p. 21)

While the ability to speak 'spontaneously' without having to refer to a script is a considerable asset for politicians, a great deal of confidence and experience is needed in order to go through with it. Unlike President Reagan, Tony Benn did not spend thirty years as a professional actor, before entering politics, and does not need to use a 'sincerity machine'. He does, however, come from a background which has moulded a large number of British orators, namely the route from the public-school debating society to the Oxford Union, of which Mr Benn was president in 1947. In his formative years, then, Mr Benn had plenty of opportunities to observe and practise the arts and crafts of oratory. And the ability to speak without referring to a script was by no means the only skill he mastered.

Combining forces

Even a fairly casual inspection of Mr Benn's speeches reveals that he makes regular use of *all* the techniques described in the previous chapters. He also has the capacity to combine many of them together in the course of producing a single claptrap. This strategy is particularly important when it comes to divided audiences, in which there are both supporters and opponents. Under these circumstances, the challenge for the speaker is to make sure that as many as possible of his own supporters come in on cue with a suitably enthusiastic display of approval. If this is done successfully, it will then look as though there is strong backing for his assertions. A favourable response of adequate duration and intensity should also have the effect of drowning out any signs of dissent from opposing factions in the audience. By using several devices at the same time, all of which point in the same direction, a speaker is able to maximize the chances of all his supporters noticing at least one of them and thus applauding when the time comes.

At the 1980 Labour Party conference, Mr Benn made a major speech in favour of various constitutional reforms relating to the inclusion of policies in election manifestoes. Part of his argument involved an attack on his former colleagues in the Wilson and Callaghan governments, some of whom were sitting alongside him on the platform as he made the speech. The television crew covering the event were therefore able to show close-ups of Mr Callaghan shaking his head and mouthing words like 'No' and 'Not true' while Mr Benn's supporters in the hall applauded each successive attack. One of these is reproduced as extract (43) which, in the light of what was demonstrated in earlier chapters, can be viewed as a technical masterpiece. Thus, Mr Benn gives advance notice that he is about to say something important, and then proceeds to use almost every device in the book to package a multi-dimensional attack.

In this short sequence, Mr Benn manages to insult 'them' on several different counts: 'they' are opposed to policies approved of by conference, make no effort to argue their position openly, wait until they are safely behind closed doors and then exploit their power of veto to get what they want. It would be extremely difficult for any of Mr Benn's supporters in the audience to miss noticing every one of these insulting dimensions and consequently not to realize that an applaudable message was being delivered.

In packaging the message, Mr Benn also takes no chances

when it comes to projecting a completion point. He deploys a
contrast, the second part of which ends with a three-part list.
Such combined usage of these two main types of verbal format
is comparatively rare, but it is an extremely effective way of
constructing an applaudable message (as will be seen again in
the next chapter). This is particularly so when the two parts of
the contrast are clearly marked out by different and carefully
timed gestures. During the first part of the contrast in extract
(43), Mr Benn points forward with his left hand on each of the
stressed beats. This pointing gesture stops just after he begins
on the second part, when his right hand moves up from his
side in time for him to thump his left hand with a clenched fist
at the exact moment when he says the word 'kill' (see plate
4.3). An obviously aggressive gesture is thus perfectly timed to
coincide with the delivery of an aggressive word. But no
applause occurs at this point, as he signals continuation both
with a rise in intonation and an upward movement of his fist.
Three further thumps smack out the beat on the stressed
syllables in '<u>SEC</u>RETLY', '<u>PRI</u>VATELY' and 'with<u>out</u>'. Completion is then indicated when the third item in the list is delivered

4.3 Mr Benn combines several devices to build a multiple attack on his former colleagues, whereupon the TV picture switches to one of them.

'... Those who oppose policies don't bother to argue with conference ...'

'... because they wait to the Clause Five meeting ...'

'... and they ...'

'... *kill* it ...'

'... secretly, privately, without debate.'

(Picture cuts to one of the accused.)

with falling intonation and at a lower volume than the previous two. In addition, Mr Benn shows no sign of continuing with any more thumping gestures. Given this veritable barrage of finely timed and co-ordinated techniques, it is hardly surprising that his supporters start to applaud immediately after the third item in the list, even though it was not projected to be the last by a preceding 'and'.

If this message is such a skilfully packaged one that Mr Benn's supporters are left in no doubt both *that* they should applaud and *when* they should start doing so, it may seem rather curious that he continues to speak *after* a completion point that had been so clearly projected. And the applause, it will be noted, overlaps not with the concluding few words of the message (as was seen in many of the extracts in earlier chapters), but with the beginning of something new. Shortly after indicating that he is going on to make another point (by saying 'now . . .'), Mr Benn breaks off in the middle of the word 'resentment'. This turns out to be the first of several attempts to continue, each one of which progresses a little further than the last:

---

(43) (continuation)

Benn: . . . with ↓ <u>out</u> ↓ de<u>bate</u> ⌈now MY RESENT (0.5)⌉ =
Audience: ⌊ x-xxXXXXXXXXX ⌋

Benn: = ⌈my re<u>sent</u>ment (2.0) my re<u>sent</u>ment about⌉ =
Audience: = ⌊XXXXXXXXXXXXXXXXXXX<u>XXXXXXXXXXXXX</u>⌋

Benn: = ⌈the uh— (0.5) my resentment about the⌉ =
Audience: = ⌊XXXXXXxxxxxxxxxxxxxxxxxxxxxxxxxxxxx⌋

Benn: = ⌈exclusion of the House⌉ of Lords and . . .
Audience: = ⌊xxxxxxxxxxxxxxxxxxx-x⌋

What Mr Benn does here is not an isolated example of his craft. Indeed, so frequently does he carry on talking after the audience response has started that it can be regarded as a standard part of his routine – to the extent that in some of his speeches he continues to talk in overlap with every single burst of applause. This strategy is all the more interesting because Mr Benn is the only contemporary British politician who makes such regular use of it. There are various reasons for supposing that it is critically important when it comes to achieving recognition as a spellbinding orator.

Refusing invited applause

By making no attempt to carry on until after a burst of applause has died away, the majority of public speakers in effect acknowledge that such a response was indeed the appropriate thing for the audience to have done. In this way, they can be said to be 'accepting' the display of approval they had just invited. Conversely, a speaker who tries to continue in the face of mounting applause effectively 'refuses' to accept it. The fact that he carried on suggests that the response had not been expected, has come as a complete surprise and had certainly not been elicited. This has three immediate consequences, all of which are to the speaker's advantage. The first is that if he did not invite the applause, then it must have been a purely spontaneous response from the audience. Secondly, if the speaker did nothing to prompt and will not accept the applause, he must be a less devious and more modest person than those who do both. Thirdly, by trying to carry on with his speech, he demonstrates that he considers the development of his argument to be more important than waiting around to accept (or savour) the plaudits of the crowd. In other words, he will appear to be passionately committed to the business of getting his point across, as well as reluctant to accept praise.

The favourable impression created by the failure of the first attempt to continue is augmented by further attempts. Repeatedly breaking off in mid-sentence makes it appear that he is having to struggle to make himself heard against a burst of applause that is now well under way and has reached maximum intensity. The impression is created that he or his message is so popular with the audience that he is in serious danger of being drowned out by their uncontrollable enthusiasm.

Close observation, however, reveals that Mr Benn's control over the situation is no less complete than that displayed by comedians, such as Frankie Howerd, who incite their audiences to further laughter by trying to stop them laughing. For the fact that Mr Benn and his audience start to compete with each other to make themselves heard is initiated in the first place by the speaker himself, not by the audience. It is, after all, he who gives them every reason to start clapping, and who then tries to interrupt in the midst of the applause. Various other aspects of Mr Benn's performance also show that his behaviour is carefully aligned with and continually responsive to that of his audience. Having not blinked his eyes at all during the delivery of the claptrap, the first blink comes a split second after the first clap is heard. Then, as he continues to speak, he raises his voice (indicated by capital letters in the transcript) in response to the increasing intensity of the applause. Subsequently, his restarts are only repeated until such time as the level of applause has started to decline (shown by small x's in the transcript), whereupon he proceeds into the clear with no further hesitations. His delivery can thus be seen to be precisely timed to ensure that there is no danger of his audience failing to hear the beginning of his next point.

If it does not matter whether the audience actually hears what he says, Mr Benn abandons the repeated restart technique in favour of moving forward to completion. A simple case of this was extract (22), which is also another fine example of the combined deployment of several devices at once. The speech is concluded with a seven-part list which turns out to be the first part of a contrast between the democratic practices of the party at large and the undemocratic behaviour of its leaders. The items in the list are marked by double-handed prodding gestures, and the second part of the contrast is delivered more slowly and is accompanied by a different single-handed patting gesture. The applause starts before he finishes the last word of the contrast, and all that is left for Mr Benn to add is the formal concluding statement. As there is obviously nothing to be lost if no one hears him say 'Comrades I invite you to support this motion', he can safely proceed right through to completion without any hesitations or restarts.

Similar fluency in the face of competing applause is also found when the applause starts so early as to be a clear sign that the audience has anticipated what the message is going to be. This is what happened in the passage for which Mr Benn's famous 'Thousand peers' speech is named, and which is reproduced here as extract (44).

(22) (Labour Party conference, 1980)

Benn: . . . I have been responsible now for five

(A)→
- ①→years to see the policies develop in the sub-committees,
- ②→come to the executive,
- ③→be discussed,
- ④→go to the unions for consultation,
- ⑤→be discussed in the liaison committee with the unions,
- ⑥→come to conference,
- ⑦→be endorsed,

(0.5)

(B)→ and then I have seen them cast aside in secret by those who are not accountable to this movement. Comrades I invite you

Audience: x-xxXXXXXXXXXXXXXXXXXXXXX =

Benn: = to support this motion

Audience: XXXXXXXXXXXXX XXXX . . . (standing ovation)

---

(44) (Labour Party conference, 1980)

Benn: . . . an immediate bill is to do what the movement has wanted to do (.) for a HUNDRED

Audience: x-xxXXXXXXXXXXXXXXX =

Benn: = YEARS (0.7) AND TO GET RID OF THE HOUSE

Audience: XXXXXXXXXXXXXXXXXXXXXXXXXXXX =

Benn: = OF LORDS (0.5) AND IF I MAY SAY SO (2.0)

Audience: XXXXXXXXXXXXXXXXXXXXXXXXXXXXXX =

Benn: = WE SHALL HAVE TO DO IT (3.0) WE SHALL

Audience: XXXXXXXXXXXXXXXXXXXXXXXXXXXXX =

Benn: = HAVE TO DO IT (0.5) BY UHH BY CREATING

Audience: XXXXXXXXXXXXXXXXxxxxxxxxxxxxxxxx =

Benn: = A THOUSAND PEERS AND THEN =

Audience: xxxxxxxxx-x

Benn: = ABOLISHING the peerage as well (.) at the time that the bill goes through . . . (TV editor's cut)

In this case, the applause started quite a long way before Mr
Benn had actually recommended abolition of the House of

Lords. He was presumably able to conclude from this that the audience had accurately guessed what he was about to say, and hence that it would hardly matter if the rest of his message were to be drowned out by the clapping. It was therefore safe enough for him to continue through to 'get rid of the House of Lords' without any hesitations or restarts. Immediately afterwards, however, this confident fluency is abandoned – just at the point where he is about to start describing how abolition is to be achieved. This is new material and he cannot rely on the audience being able to guess what it will contain. As the applause is still very loud, there is the risk that no one will hear what he says next. Rather than shutting up altogether, Mr Benn resorts to the use of a filler which merely requests permission to continue ('and if I may say so'). This is then followed by repeated restarts similar to those used in extract (43), and fluency is resumed only when the intensity of the applause has declined to a low enough level for him to be sure of being heard.

To this point, it has been observed that Mr Benn not only makes regular use of the main techniques for eliciting applause, but also frequently carries on talking after it has started. As well as helping to give the impression that he is so popular that he can't make himself heard above the acclaim, speaking in competition with applause also tends to cause it to die down sooner than it might otherwise have done. One of the things that can then be done is to produce yet another claptrap, so that more applause follows in quick succession. An example of this being done repeatedly is provided in extract (45), which is a quite extraordinary specimen of sustained technical virtuosity.

After a comparison between the task before the Labour Party and that faced by the Attlee government of 1945, Mr Benn produces a dramatic contrast in which the Conservative record is attacked by means of a comparison with that of Nazi Germany. During the applause which follows, he carries on talking, but only to say things that can be safely ignored. Once in the clear, he delivers a rhetorical question which contrasts 'our' language with 'their' economic jargon. He then talks through the ensuing flutter of applause to produce yet another contrast, whereupon the audience responds on cue. Half a second later, Mr Benn is off again and, after a further pause and hesitation, proceeds to contrast cuts in money for kidney machines with expenditure on nuclear weapons.

(45) (Labour Party special conference, May 1980)

Benn: Comrades when we return to power we shall inherit (0.4) a situation (0.2) as critical as (0.2) the nineteen forty five Labour Government.

            (0.8)

Ⓐ→ Then there were three million (0.4) men and women in the services who had to be demobilized and put back into industry Hitler had tried to destroy by bombing.

            (1.0)

Ⓑ→ We shall find two or three million (0.8) demoralized long term unemployed (0.8) who have to be put back to work in factories

    Ⓐ→(.) NOT THAT HITLER HAS BOMBED

         (.)

    Ⓑ→BUT THAT THATCHER AND JOSEPH HAVE CLOSED. (0.5) ⌈AND IT WILL⌉=

Audience: ⌊x-x-XXXXXX⌋

Benn: =⌈BE A MAJOR TASK (0.4) that we⌉=

Audience: ⌊XXXXXXXXXXXXXXXXXXXXXXXXX⌋

Benn: =⌈have to undertake (1.8) AND MAY I⌉=

Audience: ⌊XXXXXXXXXXXXXXXXXXXXXXXX⌋

Benn: =⌈SAY   UH—(0.4)   SOMETHING⌉=

Audience: ⌊XXXXXxxxxxxxxxxxxxxxxxxxxxxx⌋

Benn: =⌈UH—VERY SIMPLE (0.8)⌉

Audience: ⌊xxxxxxxxxxxxxxx-x-x⌋

Benn: Ⓐ→Is it not perhaps time we spoke in language that extended a bit beyond (0.2)

    Ⓑ→the economic jargon that has been the curse of so much of the post war years
         ⌈I AM WAITING FOR⌉

Audience: ⌊x-xxxxxxxxxxxx-x-x⌋

Benn: US TO SAY MORE OFTEN

         (0.8)

    Ⓐ→THAT SOME THINGS ARE RIGHT

         (.)

```
        Ⓑ→AND  SOME  THINGS  ARE  WRONG
              ⌈(0.5) THAT IT IS WRONG (0.8) TO⌉
Audience:     ⌊x-xxXXXXXXXXXXXXXXXXXXXXXX⌋=
Benn:        =⌈UH—UH—CUT  DOWN  ON  MONEY⌉=
Audience:     ⌊XXXXXXXXXXXXXXXXxxxxxxxxxxx⌋
Benn:     Ⓐ≥⌈FOR   KIDNEY  MACHINES⌉  AND=
Audience:    ⌊xxxxxxxxxxxxxxxxxxxx-x-x⌋
Benn:        Ⓑ→SPEND  FIVE  BILLION  ON  A  NEW
              POLARIS  SUBMARINE ⌈THAT IT IS⌉=
Audience:                        ⌊Hear hear  ⌋
                                   x-x-xxXX
Benn:        =⌈WRONG (0.8) TO DO MANY OF THE⌉=
Audience:     ⌊XXXXXXXXXXXXXXXXXXXXXXXXX⌋=
Benn:        =⌈THINGS THAT ARE NOW DONE⌉ in the
Audience:     ⌊XXXXxxxxxxxxxxxxxxxxxxxx-x-x⌋
Benn:         interests  of  profit  and  loss  .... (TV
              editor's cut)
```

This 'rapid fire' technique involves following one claptrap with another in quick succession. Each time the audience responds, the amount of clapping is cut short as the speaker continues to talk in competition with it. The audience is thus prevented from producing anything like a full eight seconds worth of applause, and is effectively 'bottled up' in such a way that everyone will be almost literally bursting to clap again at the next possible opportunity. In extract (45), another opportunity repeatedly arises more or less immediately. In this way, the audience is given a powerful incentive for sustaining a heightened level of attentiveness. It is difficult to get a sense from the transcript alone of how this particular excerpt sounds, but the original sequence created an atmosphere so electrifying that it is almost possible to visualize people sitting on the edge of their seats, ready and eager to produce a full-blooded show of approval.

It has been seen that Mr Benn is not only able to speak without a script, and to deploy all the major techniques for delivering a successful claptrap, often running many of them together in a single sequence, but is also almost alone among contemporary British politicians in his mastery of another set of techniques for responding to applause once it has started. The effects of these are almost entirely beneficial from the point of view of establishing a reputation as a spellbinding orator. When a speaker continues to talk in competition with the applause, it looks as though he is so popular that he is having to struggle to make himself heard. Meanwhile, those in the audience find themselves engaged in a more direct form of two-way communication than is the case when listening to more ordinary orators. They are put in a position of having to search actively for opportunities to produce a fully fledged display of approval. Their participation is thus more like that found in small-scale conversational settings, where turns as speakers and listeners alternate with similar rapidity.

John F. Kennedy and Martin Luther King

While Mr Benn has a near monopoly over the use of these techniques on the contemporary British scene, he is not the only politician ever to have used them. However, the skill of talking into the applause does appear to be a rare commodity in the field of political oratory. Since the present study began, only two others who possessed it have been identified, namely John F. Kennedy and Martin Luther King. And the fact that they were two of the most unquestionably 'charismatic' speakers of the post-war period strongly supports the suggestion that this particular form of technical skill is an important factor in achieving recognition as a spellbinding orator. The connection between Kennedy's use of the strategy and his ability to convey a 'sense of passion and conviction' was thus commented on in a *New York Times* article comparing the styles of the two presidential candidates in the 1960 campaign:

> When the crowds start to applaud, he [Kennedy] is often carried by his own momentum through the first outburst smothering the uproar. For all this, his platform style conveys a sense of passion and conviction that seems to reach the crowd, even when his reasoning is lost. (*New York Times*, 25 September 1960)

If the journalist who wrote this had looked more closely at what Kennedy actually said after the applause had started, he might well have discovered that, as in the case of Mr Benn, there was little chance of his reasoning being lost.

105

4.4   John F. Kennedy and Martin Luther King were two other highly effective orators who regularly talked during bursts of applause.

The same strategy was also mentioned in an article on Martin Luther King in the magazine *Encounter*, where it was referred to as 'biting into' the audience responses. As can be seen below, the author singled this out from 'every device ever contrived by every preacher of the South' as having played an important part in contributing to the impressiveness of King's celebrated 'I have a dream' speech. Not mentioned, however, is another device which was also much in evidence, for contrasts also feature repeatedly in the extracts from the speech selected for direct quotation:

In the most famous passage of his most famous speech, before the Lincoln Memorial in Washington, in 1963, three centuries of the rhetoric of the South were pulled together into one exalted outburst. Every device ever contrived by every preacher of the South, black or white, was put to use, until his huge audience, black and white, had been carried beyond itself, no longer merely the sum of its members. He bit into the gathering Amens, the answering 'Yeah! Yeah!', the thundering applause, for they were not to be allowed to rest, but were to be carried to a higher pitch with each ejaculation. It went like this.

I have a dream that one day even the State of Mississippi, a
    desert sweltering with the heat of injustice and oppression
'Yeah! Yeah!' –

will be transformed into an oasis of freedom and justice.
– the Amens roll into the rising applause. He does not let them die:

I have a dream that my four little children
– 'Amen! Amen!' 'Yeah! Yeah!' –

will one day live in a nation where they will not be judged
by the colour of their skin but by the content of their
character
– the Amens and the applause swell. But he bites into them:
    I have a dream today
The applause rises, held now in anticipation of what is to come:

I have a dream that one day the State of Alabama....
And so on, until he bites again into the applause, with the reiterated, 'I have a dream today,' as he carried the audience to the final:

I have a dream that one day every valley shall be exalted, every hill and mountain will be made low, the rough places will be made plain, and the crooked places will be made straight, and the glory of the Lord shall be revealed, and all flesh shall see it together. (Henry Fairlie, 'Martin Luther King', *Encounter*, June 1968, p.4)

Fifteen years after Martin Luther King was assassinated, a half-page article in the *Guardian* newspaper was published under the heading 'A view from the clouded mountain top'. The title was taken from a famous extract from the end of his last-ever speech, which was reprinted at the beginning of the article as follows:

'I've been to the mountain top. I've looked over and seen the promised land. I may not get there with you, but I want you to know that we as a people will get to the promised land. So I'm happy tonight.' This was Martin Luther King speaking in Memphis 15 years ago. The next day he was shot dead.... (Paul Oestreicher, *Guardian*, 4 April 1983)

The presence of a three-part list and a contrast are clear enough but the reproduction of the quotation in this form fails to convey much of a sense for the range of responses that are such an important characteristic of the black church services in the southern United States. As was pointed out in the earlier *Encounter* article, these were crucial to Martin Luther King's style of oratory. Frequent cries of 'Amen', 'Holy' and 'Yeah' made his speeches sound even more like two-way conversations with the audience than Mr Benn's rapid-fire contrast–response sequences. To perform their part in the dialogue, King's audiences must have been continually on the look-out for opportunities to respond. They must also therefore have had to concentrate very closely on everything he said. Had they not sustained a heightened level of attentiveness, his audiences would have been incapable of participating in the vibrant manner so typical of southern black congregations.

Because of the frequency and range of these audience responses, together with Martin Luther King's own extensive use of variations in volume, intonation and rhythm, it is virtually impossible to transcribe his speeches in a way that is both accurate and readable. Extract (46) has therefore been greatly simplified, but at least gives some idea of the frequency and positioning of the responses which occurred during the excerpt quoted in the *Guardian*.

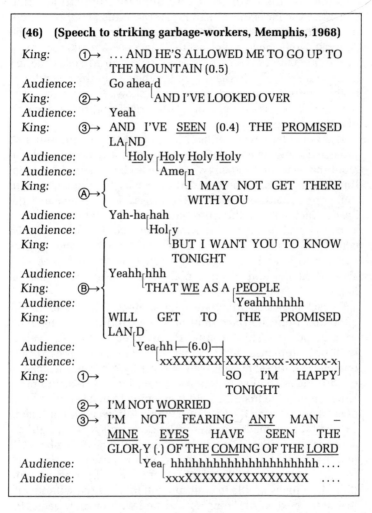

(46)   (Speech to striking garbage-workers, Memphis, 1968)

King:	①→	... AND HE'S ALLOWED ME TO GO UP TO THE MOUNTAIN (0.5)
Audience:		Go ahea⌐d
King:	②→	⌊AND I'VE LOOKED OVER
Audience:		Yeah
King:	③→	AND I'VE <u>SEEN</u> (0.4) THE <u>PROMISED</u> LA⌐ND
Audience:		⌊<u>Holy</u> ⌐<u>Holy</u> <u>Holy</u> <u>Holy</u>
Audience:		⌊Ame⌐n
King:	Ⓐ→	⌊I MAY NOT GET THERE WITH YOU
Audience:		Yah-ha⌐hah
Audience:		⌊Hol⌐y
King:		⌊BUT I WANT YOU TO KNOW TONIGHT
Audience:		Yeahh⌐hhh
King:	Ⓑ→	⌊THAT <u>WE</u> AS A ⌐<u>PEOPLE</u>
Audience:		⌊Yeahhhhhhh
King:		WILL GET TO THE PROMISED LAN⌐D
Audience:		⌊Yea⌐hh ⊢—(6.0)—⊣
Audience:		⌊xxXXXXXX⌐XXX xxxxx -xxxxxx-x⌉
King:	①→	⌊SO I'M HAPPY⌋ TONIGHT
	②→	I'M NOT <u>WORRIED</u>
	③→	I'M NOT FEARING <u>ANY</u> MAN – <u>MINE</u> <u>EYES</u> HAVE SEEN THE <u>GLOR</u>⌐Y (.) OF THE <u>COMING</u> OF THE <u>LORD</u>
Audience:		⌊Yea⌐ hhhhhhhhhhhhhhhhhhhhhhh ....
Audience:		⌊xxxXXXXXXXXXXXXXXXX ....

It is perhaps fitting that the finale of the last speech ever made by this most effective of orators was such a masterly example of

109

technical virtuosity. His gaze scanned the audience throughout, and he showed no sign at all of having a script or notes in front of him. His final declaration of faith was preceded, in quick succession by a three-part list, a contrast and another three-part list. But one thing which is very different from all the other cases cited so far is that the audience responded *after each item* in the first of the lists, and *in between* the two parts of the contrast. None the less, the fact that there was a marked increase in the intensity of the responses after the third item in the list (four 'Holy's' and an 'Amen'), and at the end of the second part of the contrast ('Yeah' and applause), shows that the audience regarded these as completion points requiring more decisive displays of approval.

The video tape reveals that Martin Luther King himself also projected these as completion points with a non-verbal movement that was not used anywhere else in the sequence. The first line and the contrast both ended in exactly the same way with the words 'promised land'. In both cases, a slight shake of the head coincided with the word 'promised'. The same head shake also occurred as he was starting to say the word 'glory', just before the final ovation got under way. The movement thus appears to have been regularly treated by the audience as a signal that the end of an applaudable message was close at hand.

Extract (46) also illustrates the strategy referred to in the quotation from the *Encounter* article as 'biting into' the audience responses. This, it appears, involved talking in overlap with the applause in a rather different and perhaps less obviously noticeable way than is done by Mr Benn. Instead of continuing as soon as a response got under way, Martin Luther King would bide his time, and then come in just before the end of each one. During the applause which followed the contrast in extract (46), he made no attempt to carry on speaking until six seconds had elapsed. And six seconds, it will be remembered, is just the point at which the intensity of applause typically starts to fall away towards the eight-second norm. By waiting until then, Dr King was able to continue totally fluently, without any fear of his next words being missed, and without any need of the repeated restarts so favoured by Mr Benn. The overall impact, however, was no less favourable, especially given that the audience responses also tended to start just before completion points were reached. When both the speaker and his audience repeatedly come in before the other has quite finished, a state of closely co-ordinated rapport exists between them, and the over-riding impression is one of intense harmony, spontaneity and mutual understanding.

Margaret Thatcher and the evolution of charismatic woman

Given that American political oratory before the 1960s had been an activity largely dominated by whites, it was important for Martin Luther King's success that there already existed a distinctive black religious tradition which could be readily adapted for speaking on behalf of the civil rights movement. For women, however, there are no such obvious models, as political oratory has been a predominantly male preserve for thousands of years. There is no record of any celebrated female orators in classical Greece or Rome, and the early texts on rhetoric and oratory were written on the assumption that the practitioners would be male. Thus, at an early stage in his mammoth work on *The Education of an Orator*, Quintillian had this to say about the aim of the book:

> We are to form, then, the perfect orator, who cannot exist unless as *a good man*; and we require in *him*, therefore, not only consummate ability in speaking, but every excellence of mind ... since the *man* who can duly sustain *his* character as a citizen, who is qualified for the management of public and private affairs, and who can govern communities by *his* counsels, settle them by means of law, and improve them by judicial enactments, can certainly be nothing else but an orator. (Quintillian, *Institutes of Oratory, or The Education of an Orator*, p. 4, emphasis added)

Recent years have seen a number of women rise to become heads of government – Mrs Bandaranaike in Sri Lanka, Mrs Perón in Argentina, Mrs Gandhi in India, Mrs Meir in Israel and Mrs Thatcher in the United Kingdom – success stories which might initially seem to suggest that the male-dominated political mould has been broken once and for all, and that women will henceforth be able to enjoy equal opportunities in the pursuit of political careers. However, there are at least two reasons for caution in drawing any such conclusion. One is that the first three in the above list of women who have achieved high political office had close family ties with *male* national heroes who had recently died. Golda Meir and Margaret Thatcher are therefore the only ones who can be said to have reached the top entirely on their own merits. A second reason for caution is that women still face a number of social and physiological obstacles with which men never have to contend. In the absence of any established tradition like that in which black American leaders have been able to operate, female politicians have to develop their own ways of surviving in a male-dominated profession. The solutions found by someone like Mrs Thatcher are therefore likely to create behavioural precedents from which aspiring female politicians of the future may be able to learn and benefit.

Some of the problems faced by women in politics are much the same as those faced by women in any other male-dominated profession. They are aptly summed up in the colloquial saying to the effect that 'women are damned if they behave like men, and damned if they don't.' Thus, if a woman acts in a tough, decisive or ruthless manner, she is likely to find her femininity being called into question. But if she is gentle, indecisive or conciliatory, her male colleagues may consider her unsuitable for the job. Such a dilemma is familiar to most professional women, but political women are confronted by additional disadvantages because public speaking is such an important part of their work. This is not just because the skills of oratory and debating have been monopolized by men for such a long time, but is also because there are differences in the length of male and female vocal cords which result in the difference in pitch of male and female voices.

Pitch can pose problems for all public speakers, whatever their sex, because it tends to rise when a speaker is nervous or speaks louder than usual, both of which are likely to happen in oratory. For women, however, the problem is more acute because the natural pitch of their voices has a higher starting-point than is the case for men, and therefore cannot rise as far before reaching a level at which it sounds excessively 'shrill'. This might not matter were it not for the fact that high-pitched vocalizations tend to be strongly associated with emotional or irrational outbursts – a deeply rooted cultural assumption that no doubt derives from, and is sustained by, the screams of each new generation of infants. The fact that the sound of a woman raising her voice is more likely to be negatively evaluated as 'shrill' or 'screeching' is probably at the heart of a source of irritation which is familiar to many professional women, namely the tendency of male colleagues to accuse them of 'over-reacting' whenever they become involved in arguments.

Consistent with such attitudes to high-pitched female vocalizations is the fact that lower-pitched female voices tend to be regarded as more attractive than high-pitched voices. There is a strong association between 'huskiness' and 'sexiness', and Shakespeare's positive evaluation of low pitch has long been enshrined in the dictionaries of quotations: 'Her voice was ever soft, gentle and low, an excellent thing in woman' (King Lear, V, iii). Viewed in these terms, the fact that Mrs Thatcher has taken positive steps to lower the pitch of her voice can be seen as a perfectly rational response to a very real problem. Under the guidance of a tutor from the National Theatre, she underwent a training programme which included special humming exercises aimed at lowering the pitch level at which she formerly spoke. From tape recordings of speeches made before and after receiving tuition a marked difference can be clearly heard. When these are played through an electronic pitch and intensity analyser, it emerges that she achieved a reduction in pitch of 46 Hz, a figure which is almost half the average difference in pitch between male and female voices. Such a decrease is all the more remarkable for the fact that it was accomplished after Mrs Thatcher had already passed the age at which the pitch of women's voices tends naturally to rise: generally speaking, a steady reduction takes place up to the age of forty-five, after which the pitch gradually rises again. The lowering of her voice has had other consequences which have probably contributed both to the greater clarity of her talk and to its 'statesmanlike' character. For example, the human voice-production system is organized in such a way that reductions in pitch involve physiological processes which tend to slow down the speed at which we speak, and Mrs Thatcher now speaks noticeably less rapidly than she did before undergoing voice tuition.

The problem of pitch is only one of several aspects of public speaking that Mrs Thatcher has taken seriously in recent years. She has received advice from other professionals in the theatre, and from those in television and even evangelism. Thus, one of her main speech-writers is Ronald Millar, a playwright about whose influence two of Mrs Thatcher's biographers have noted as follows:

> She ... turned out to be an amenable pupil to Millar's methods, which included advice on delivery as well as script. Millar has become known as the author of the jokes (he was responsible for 'U-turn if you want to – the lady's not for turning'), but his principal skill was and is playing director to the leading lady, a combination of firm steering mixed with reassurance. (Wapshott and Brock, *Thatcher*, p. 161)

'The lady's not for turning' is but one of many contrastive punch lines supplied to Mrs Thatcher by Millar, and Wapshott and Brock also report that it was at his suggestion that she quoted the following four contrasts from St Francis of Assisi as she entered Downing Street after winning the 1979 general election:

> Where there is discord, may we bring harmony.
> Where there is error, may we bring truth.
> Where there is doubt, may we bring faith.
> Where there is despair, may we bring hope.

Since before the 1979 election, television producer Gordon Reece has provided Mrs Thatcher with extensive and detailed guidance on how to perform effectively on the small screen. And during the 1983 general election, the staging of her set-piece speeches was organized by the same team that manages mass meetings for Billy Graham's evangelical crusades to Britain.

Much of this expert help, of course, has little or nothing to do with the specific problems faced by a female political leader. But some of the advice, such as that provided by Gordon Reece, has been directly concerned with 'image-related' matters like hair styles, clothes, jewellery and make-up. This has included a recommendation to go for greater simplicity of appearance in

114

television performances than when making major speeches. Reece and Millar have also paid close attention to the problems associated with pitch. To quote her biographers again:

> A full blast Commons speech can sound like raving hysteria in a broadcasting studio. The broadcasting of the Commons (which happened to coincide with Reece's arrival) caused him special problems. He was heard to remark that the selling of Margaret Thatcher had been put back two years by the mass broadcasting of Prime Minister's Question Time as she had to be at her shrillest to be heard over the din.... Millar had also taught her that lowering the voice brought the speed down to a steadier rate. He advised holding to a steady and equable tone at Question Time which would eventually drive through, not over or under, the noise. (Wapshott and Brock, *Thatcher*, pp. 169–70)

Prior to the 1979 general election, the Conservative Party's advertising agents, Saatchi and Saatchi, were also worried about the prospects of convincing the electorate of the leadership potential not just of a woman, but of one who so closely resembled a stereotypical middle-class suburban housewife. Meanwhile, the various nicknames devised by her cabinet colleagues over the past few years – 'Mother', the 'Leaderene', the 'Bossette', 'Attila the Hen', 'the Immaculate Misconception', and so on – can be viewed as reflecting a sustained attempt on their part to come to terms with the fact of having a woman as their leader. So, too, can the culturally available stereotypes of powerful women that cartoonists have regularly exploited in their caricatures of Mrs Thatcher, a selection of which includes Boadicea, Britannia, the Queen and a witch. But perhaps the most astute and informative attempt to come to terms with Mrs Thatcher's position as a political leader was supplied by the Soviet newspapers when, after a speech at Kensington Town Hall in 1976, they dubbed her the 'Iron Lady'. Of all the various nicknames Mrs Thatcher has attracted, it is as the 'Iron Lady' that she has become internationally best known. And this may well be because these two words aptly sum up one of the main secrets of her success in finding a solution to the problem of being both female and powerful.

Given that successful women face the dilemma of being 'damned if they behave like men, and damned if they don't', one solution is to behave in as efficient, tough and decisive a manner as possible, while at the same time making no concessions whatsoever in maintaining the external trappings of femininity. Thus, Mrs Thatcher is a strong believer in the importance of being smart in a conventionally feminine way, and has consistently sought to make the most of her natural physical attractiveness. This has included the preservation of her blonde hair by regular tinting and elimination of a gap in her teeth by dental capping. Nor has she been afraid to be seen in the traditional female roles of wife and mother, even to the extent of being photographed at the kitchen sink just before competing as a candidate in the 1975 Conservative Party leadership election. Her uncompromisingly feminine appearance, and her repeated emphasis on the virtues of family life have not endeared Mrs Thatcher to radical women's groups. But in the eyes and ears of a wider public, such factors have had the effect of insulating her from being 'damned' for lacking culturally acceptable feminine attributes, by leaving no one with any possible grounds for doubt that she is anything less than a 100 per cent female of the species.

In Mrs Thatcher's conduct of government there has been little that anyone has been able to single out as 'gentle' or 'weak', and this has enabled her to avoid being 'damned' for possessing the sorts of stereotypical feminine attributes so often invoked in attempts to demonstrate the unsuitability of women for positions of power and responsibility. At the same time, her external image of unambiguously recognizable femininity may have gone a long way towards freeing her to pursue forceful policies without running any risk of being damned for behaving like a man. Such allegations are so transparently at odds with all the other evidence that she is a thoroughly normal woman that they lack serious credibility. With utterances like 'A General doesn't leave the field of battle just as it's reaching a climax', she has thus been able to show no inhibitions about identifying herself closely with powerful male roles, without at the same time having to worry about whether or not this might raise doubts about her essential femininity. It is also reported that it was Mrs Thatcher herself who first used the word 'wet', a

4.5
Mrs Thatcher's
teeth before
and after
dental-capping
treatment.

colloquialism for describing men who are feeble or lacking in masculinity, to refer to her more left-wing Tory colleagues.

The aptness of the 'Iron Lady' as a nickname for Mrs Thatcher can thus be seen to derive from the way it captures the two most visible and contrasting characteristics of her public image – toughness and femininity. And it is arguably the case that, when these two qualities are exhibited in the conduct and appearance of the same woman, she will have found a workable way of deterring, resisting and neutralizing attacks based on male-chauvinist assumptions. It may therefore be no coincidence that, far from taking exception to the 'Iron Lady' label, Mrs Thatcher has apparently revelled in it, even to the extent of reminding the public of its applicability and relevance as an electoral asset some seven years after it first saw the light of day:

> **(47)   (UK general election, 1983)**
>
> *Thatcher:*   The Russians said that I was an Iron Lady.
> *Audience:*   Hear hear.
> *Thatcher:*   They were right.
> *Audience:*   Heh heh ⌈heh
> *Audience:*   ⌊xxXXXXXXXXXXXxxx (TV editor's cut)
> *Thatcher:*   Britain needs an Iron Lady.
> *Audience:*   Hear ⌈hear
> *Audience:*   ⌊xxXXXXXXX (TV editor's cut)

In a similar vein, she has not tried to deny the appropriateness of another nickname, which locates her firmly within a long-standing and culturally familiar class of successful women, namely that of 'Headmistress'. In this connection, her answer to a question put to her during the 1983 election by John Cole of the BBC reflects a clear willingness on her part to be identified with such an image. And it is interesting to note that this response came in the context of rebutting complaints formulated in fairly blatantly male-chauvinist terms:

> **(48)   (UK general election, 1983)**
>
> *Cole:*   Other Prime Ministers after all have been bossy too, but Mrs Thatcher does undoubtedly keep a fussy watch on their [her ministers'] performances with an occasional touch of motherliness. I asked her today what she said to suggestions that she had a headmistress image.
> *Thatcher:*   Well I've known some very very good headmistresses who've launched their pupils on wonderful careers. I had one such and was very very grateful. But I am what I am. Yes, my style is of vigorous leadership. Yes, I do believe certain things very strongly. Yes, I do believe in trying to persuade people that the things I believe in are the things they should follow. And Mr Cole I'm far too old to change now.

By saying not just that there is nothing wrong with being like a headmistress, but that it can have positive virtues, Mrs Thatcher was able to identify herself with one of the relatively few widely respected positions of power and responsibility which have traditionally been available to women. Teaching is also one of the very few professions where the nature of the job involves a great deal of public speaking. For a female political leader to be identified with the role of headmistress would therefore seem to be something worth cultivating as part of the business of encouraging wider acceptance of the fact that women are perfectly capable of holding their own both on public platforms and in the corridors of power.

Indeed, it is arguable that one of Mrs Thatcher's major long-term achievements will turn out to have been the undermining of age-old assumptions of the sort contained in Quintillian's observation that the perfect orator 'cannot exist unless as a good man'. And, by finding a workable solution to the problem of being damned for being like a man and damned for not, her combination of uncompromising femininity with equally un-compromising words and deeds may have laid the foundations for a new tradition within which women politicians of the future will be able to operate.

The education of a female orator

Although Mrs Thatcher has taken the business of public speaking very seriously since becoming leader of the Con-servative Party, it is important not to forget that she had already come a long way in the years before she reached high office. She must therefore have found a successful way of surviving in the male-dominated world of politics long before Ronald Millar, Gordon Reece or Saatchi and Saatchi came on the scene. In this connection, her biography is of considerable interest, because it shows that, from a very early age, the former Margaret Roberts had far more opportunities than most girls of her generation to become accustomed to being treated on equal terms with men.

Mrs Thatcher's father was very active both as a local town councillor in Grantham and as a Methodist lay preacher. According to her biographers, the young Margaret was not just exposed throughout her childhood to the political discussions which regularly took place in the Roberts household and across the counter of their corner grocery shop, but was also actively encouraged by her father to take part in them. At the same time, she was exposed to weekly Sunday sermons in the local Methodist church and, more spasmodically, listened to public speeches by national politicians who were visiting the town. Evidence that she showed early promise of putting these experiences to good use is provided by the fact that, at the age of nine, she won a poetry-reading competition at a local drama festival. It is also reported that such talents continued to blossom while she was a pupil at Kesteven and Grantham Girls' School:

> She was a studious girl, but enjoyed the dramatic society, which made her at one time consider becoming an actress, and also question and answer sessions at the end of visitors' lectures, as long as the subject was current affairs. She is well remembered by a girl in the year above her, Margaret Goodrich, for cross-questioning Bernard Newman, the expert on spying, with a confidence not normally expected from such a young girl. (Wapshott and Brock, *Thatcher*, pp. 34–5)

For her higher education, the future prime minister could hardly have selected a university more dominated by men and male traditions than the Oxford of the 1940s. Nor could she have chosen a subject studied by fewer women or by fewer aspiring politicians than chemistry – Mrs Thatcher is not just the first woman, but also the first scientist, to have become prime minister. At the same time, part of the experience of living in a segregated all women's college for three years involved taking it for granted that women academics were perfectly capable of performing on equal terms with men. Thus, her chemistry tutor at Somerville was Dorothy Hodgkin, who subsequently went on to win a Nobel prize. During this period she also kept up an active interest in politics, and became president of the University Conservative Association, a post which brought her into direct contact with many of the then leading national politicians, as well as her own student contemporaries who were later to achieve cabinet rank (including Tony Benn, Anthony Crosland and Edward Boyle).

In her subsequent careers, first as an industrial research chemist and later as a tax barrister, Mrs Thatcher continued to live and work on equal terms with men in professions where women were still extremely under-represented. By the time she won a seat in parliament, she had therefore already accumulated two decades of experience at participating in male-dominated environments. Even allowing for the inevitable tendency of biographers and obituary-writers to select facts from a life story which fit in with whatever the subject eventually became, it would seem that Mrs Thatcher underwent a lengthy and highly relevant apprenticeship, similar to that recommended by the classical Greek and Roman experts on the education of male orators. As can be seen in the excerpts from her speeches discussed in other chapters, there is no doubt of her ability to deploy the full range of rhetorical devices, and to do so in such a way that her essential femininity can never be seriously called into question.

Charisma as method

Words like 'spellbinding' and 'charisma' suggest that some political orators are capable of bewitching or mesmerizing their audiences. They reflect the traditional view that such people are not like ordinary mortals, but are possessed of magical powers or supernatural gifts which are so mysterious as to defy description. However, by looking closely at spellbinding oratory in action, it emerges that there is nothing particularly mysterious about it, and that it involves the mastery of a relatively small number of *technical* skills that can be identified and described. Some of these are the basic techniques that are widely used by all politicians for eliciting favourable responses, but outstanding orators also have the ability to use them in quick succession, and to combine a variety of carefully co-ordinated verbal, non-verbal, intonational and rhythmic signals in the production of an invitation to applaud – and to do so without having to refer to a script. Another important weapon in their armoury, which is hardly ever deployed by lesser orators, is that of speaking in overlap with the applause. As has been seen, this can be done in a number of different ways, all of which work to enhance the favourable impact made on the

121

audience with whom the speaker is interacting.

The long-standing domination of western politics by white males means that others, such as blacks and women, have to overcome special obstacles in order to be taken seriously by wider audiences. The experiences of Martin Luther King and more recent civil rights leaders like Jesse Jackson suggest that for the moment black Americans can successfully operate within the framework provided by the established traditions and practices of their own southern churches. But women are still in the position of having to break new ground when it comes to finding an effective *modus operandi*, and it would seem that Mrs Thatcher's solution has been to combine tough words and deeds with an otherwise uncompromisingly feminine image. A measure of her success is that, were there any doubts at all about her essential femininity, assessments such as the following would be far too delicate to be aired in public by any of her supporters, let alone by other women:

---

(49) (UK general election, 1983)

Interviewer: Can we ask you what you think of Mrs Thatcher?

Woman 1: Marvellous, absolutely fantastic. Best man in England.

Woman 2: I think she's just wonderful. The only man in parliament.

Woman 3: Great. The best man in the country.

For both blacks and women, however, the currently workable solutions are probably no more than short- to medium-term staging posts on the long route to full emancipation. Genuine equality of political opportunity will only be reached when a modified version of part of Martin Luther King's dream becomes a reality: when blacks and women are judged not by the colour or softness of their skin, but by the content of their characters.

Finally, it must be noted that there is at least one important feature of exceptional public speaking that is more difficult to characterize precisely in terms of a particular method. This is the ability to say something at just the right time to just the right audience in just the right place, an ability which seems to have been at the heart of the most memorable speeches made during the past quarter of a century. Thus, when middle-aged British adults are asked to name the most notable speeches from this period, there are five which are mentioned with extraordinary regularity: 'The wind of change' by Harold Macmillan, 'Ich bin ein Berliner' by John F. Kennedy, 'Vive Quebec libre' by Charles de Gaulle, 'I have a dream' by Martin Luther King and the 'Rivers of blood' by Enoch Powell.

In each of these cases, the speakers articulated sentiments which caught the mood of the audiences they were addressing with much greater than average precision. 'A wind of change is blowing over this continent' was said by Macmillan not just during a period of rapidly accelerating decolonization, but to members of the South African parliament. 'Ich bin ein Berliner' was one of the few statements in German that Kennedy addressed to a crowd of 150,000 in Berlin, during a visit when he became the first US president to see the then recently constructed wall dividing the city. De Gaulle's 'Vive Quebec libre' was the finale to a speech made in the heart of French Canada at a time of growing support for the separatist movement. Martin Luther King's 'I have a dream' invoked the 'American dream' on behalf of the country's black citizens at a time when the civil rights movement had established itself as a major political force, and from the Lincoln Memorial in Washington, a powerful symbol of the principles represented by that dream. And Enoch Powell's speech on immigration, in which he observed 'I seem to see the River Tiber foaming with much blood', was also made in 1968, when the Race Relations Bill, reflecting growing public concern for the issue, was before parliament. By delivering it in Birmingham, he selected a city which had attracted mass immigration from the 'new' Commonwealth countries, and which therefore had direct experience of the problems discussed in the speech.

The observations reported in this chapter do not bear directly on how speakers sometimes put their fingers on the pulse of an audience, though they do perhaps provide guidance as to how such sentiments, once identified, can be most effectively formulated and delivered.

5   Quotability

The selection and survival of quotations

Mr Neil Kinnock's first keynote address as leader of the Labour
Party included a long section attacking Conservative policies on
the welfare state. He began it by quoting from a speech Mrs
Thatcher had made the previous weekend and, as can be seen
from extract (6), the particular excerpt he selected was formulated by means of a contrast and a three-part list. Mr Kinnock
then proceeded to use the second part (i.e. the punch line) of
Mrs Thatcher's contrast as the basis for a series of rhetorical
questions, which he eventually answered with a revised version
of Mrs Thatcher's original contrast – whereupon the audience
promptly applauded on cue.

(6)   (Labour Party conference, 1983)

Kinnock: Last week in Canada (1.0) the prime minister
                      had this to say on the welfare state. (1.0) It
    Ⓐ→   might she said (0.7) end up not succouring
                      (0.5)
    Ⓑ→   but suffocating
                      (0.5)
                      and then she said
                      (0.2)
    ①→   energy is sapped
    ②→   initiative is stifled
    ③→   enterprise is destroyed
                      I ask ...

                      Are our senior citizens in Britain being suffo-
                      cated (0.2) by a pension from November of
                      thirty four pounds and five p a week?
                      (0.8)
                      I ask (0.5) are the seven million of our
                      countrymen and women (0.5) in poverty
                      being suffocated (0.5) by (0.2) their sup-
                      plementary benefits?
                      (1.0)
                      I ask if the young people who in this country
                      are (.) lucky enough (.) to get on the youth
                      training scheme are being suffocated (0.2) by
                      the paltry twenty five pounds a week.
                      (0.7)
                      Are their unemployed (0.2) contemporaries
                      being suffocated (0.5) by the fifteen and
                      sixteen and seventeen pounds a week (0.2)
                      soon to be cut according to the government?
                      (1.0)
    Ⓐ→   { I say that these people are not being suffo-
          { cated by care
                      (0.7)
    Ⓑ→   { they are being smothered by neglect
          { ⌈by the contempt of a cruel government.
Audience: ⌊x-xxXXXXXXXXXXXXXXXXXXX ....

Two years earlier, Conservative MP Norman St John-Stevas had quoted another contrast from something said by Mrs Thatcher, and claimed that it had remained in his mind not just for a week, but for the previous two and a half years:

---

(50) (Norman St John-Stevas, letter to *The Times*, 28 October 1981)

I recall [Mrs Thatcher's] brilliant television broadcast of January 17, 1979, which was such an important contribution to our subsequent election victory, when she concluded with the moving words: 'We shall have to learn again to be one nation or one day we shall be no nation.' Such an arresting antithesis has remained in my mind ever since....

Messrs Kinnock and St John-Stevas are by no means alone in their capacity to notice, remember and quote messages formulated by means of verbal formats which regularly prompt applause. Thus, many of the best-known passages from Martin Luther King's 'I have a dream...' speech involved contrasts, several of which were selected for quotation by the author of the *Encounter* article mentioned in the previous chapter. The following example was the only excerpt quoted from the speech in a feature on BBC Television's *Newsnight* twenty years later:

---

(51)   (Speech from the Lincoln Memorial, Washington, 1963)

King: I have a dream that one day
         Ⓐ→ { my four little children will not be judged
               by the colour of their skin
         Ⓑ→ but by the content of their character....

Two of the best-remembered quotations from John F. Kennedy's speeches were also packaged by means of contrasts:

---

(52)   (Inaugural address as US president, 1961)

Kennedy: Ⓐ→Ask not what your country can do for you.
          Ⓑ→Ask what you can do for your country.

> **(53) (Speech in the City Square, West Berlin, 1963)**
>
> *Kennedy:* Ⓐ→ { Two thousand years ago the proudest boast was 'Civis Romanus sum.'
>
> Ⓑ→ { Today, in the world of freedom, the proudest boast is 'Ich bin ein Berliner.'

A century earlier, one of Kennedy's predecessors as president had produced a particularly memorable three-part list:

> **(54) (Gettysburg Address, 1863)**
>
> *Lincoln:* ①→Government of the people,
> ②→by the people,
> ③→for the people.

The best-remembered extract from Winston Churchill's wartime speeches is almost certainly his assessment of the battle of Britain fighter pilots. It was concluded with a three-part list, the third item of which *contrasted* with the first two, a combined format of the sort which, as noted earlier, is comparatively rarely used:

> **(55) (House of Commons, 1940)**
>
> *Churchill:*   Never in the field of human conflict has
> Ⓐ→ { ①→ so much been owed by
> { ②→ so many to
> Ⓑ→   ③→ so few

Another well-known quotation from Churchill involved an even more complicated combination of contrastive and three-part verbal formats:

(56)   (Mansion House, 1942)

Churchill: Ⓐ→ ⎰ Ⓐ→①→ This is not the end.
            ⎱ Ⓑ→②→ It is not even the beginning of the end,
         Ⓑ→   ③→ but it is perhaps the end of the
                       beginning.

Much more recently, a similarly complex deployment of interlocking devices achieved lasting memorability for Brian Hanrahan, the BBC Television News reporter who accompanied the British task force on the Falklands campaign:

(57)   (Report from HMS *Hermes*, BBC Television News, 1982)

Hanrahan: Ⓐ→   ①→ ⎰ I'm not allowed to say how many
                       ⎱ planes were involved in the raid
          Ⓑ→ ⎰ Ⓐ→②→ but I counted them all out,
               ⎱ Ⓑ→③→ and I counted them all back

Neil Armstrong's first words on the moon were also packaged as a contrast:

(58)   (Moon broadcast, 1969)

Armstrong: Ⓐ→That's one small step for man.
              Ⓑ→One giant leap for mankind.

Contrasts and three-part lists also feature in two of the best-known quotations from the whole of English literature:

(59)   (Shakespeare, *Hamlet*, III, i)

Hamlet: Ⓐ→To be, or
           Ⓑ→not to be –
              That is the question.

> **(60) (Shakespeare, *Julius Caesar*, III, iii)**
>
> *Mark Antony:* ①→Friends,
> ②→Romans,
> ③→Countrymen,
>   lend me your ears;
> Ⓐ→I come to bury Caesar,
> Ⓑ→not to praise him.
> Ⓐ→The evil that men do lives after them;
> Ⓑ→The good is oft interred with their bones.

More recently, George Orwell created two memorable contrastive slogans in *Animal Farm*:

> **(61) (George Orwell, *Animal Farm*, 1945)**
>
> Ⓐ→All animals are equal,
> Ⓑ→but some animals are more equal than others.
> Ⓐ→Four legs good,
> Ⓑ→two legs bad.

And the party slogan in *Nineteen Eighty-Four* comprised a list of three contrasts:

> **(62) (George Orwell, *Nineteen Eighty-Four*, 1949)**
>
> ①→Ⓐ→Ⓑ→War is peace
> ②→Ⓐ→Ⓑ→Freedom is slavery
> ③→Ⓐ→Ⓑ→Ignorance is strength

Political philosophers in the real world have also shown a remarkable capacity to produce memorable contrasts:

> **(63) (Jean-Jacques Rousseau, *The Social Contract*, 1762)**
>
> Ⓐ→Man is born free and
> Ⓑ→everywhere is in chains

This sentiment was echoed nearly a century later in the contrast that precedes the final rallying cry of *The Communist Manifesto*:

---

(64) **(Karl Marx and Friedrich Engels, *The Communist Manifesto*, 1848)**

Ⓐ→ The proletarians have nothing to lose but their chains.
Ⓑ→ They have a world to win.
Workingmen of all countries, unite!

It is also the case that there are a number of three-part political and religious quotations which even linguistically untalented native speakers of English are often able to quote in the original foreign languages:

(65)	Veni, vidi, vici. (I came, I saw, I conquered.)
(66)	In nomine Patris et Filii et Spiritus Sancti. (In the name of the Father and of the Son and of the Holy Ghost.)
(67)	Liberté, egalité, fraternité. (Liberty, equality, fraternity.)
(68)	Ein Volk, ein Reich, ein Führer. (One people, one state, one leader.)

Sometimes, as with Kennedy's 'Ich bin ein Berliner' (extract 53), it is only the second part of a contrast which survives, in which case it may have to be slightly modified in order to stand on its own. 'On your bike' has thus come to be regarded in the minds of his critics as Tory cabinet minister Norman Tebbit's advice to the unemployed. However, this translation into a colloquial expression of abuse actually originated in the second part of a contrast:

> **(69) (Conservative Party conference, 1981)**
>
> *Tebbit:* Ⓐ→My father didn't riot,
>   Ⓑ→he got on his bike and he looked for work.

Similarly, 'Hell hath no fury like a woman scorned' was widely quoted when another Tory cabinet minister, Cecil Parkinson, resigned after the details of his extra-marital affair with a secretary had become a matter of public debate. But in the original version it was phrased slightly differently as part of a contrast between heaven and hell. As with 'on your bike', some revision has been involved in making the second part coherent on its own:

> **(70) (Congreve, *The Mourning Bride*, III)**
>
> *Zara:* Ⓐ Heaven has no rage like love to hatred turned,
>   Ⓑ Nor Hell a fury like a woman scorned.

These various examples from diverse sources and historical periods show that messages packaged as contrasts and three-part lists have a remarkable capacity for evoking responses far beyond the audiences to whom they were originally delivered. The fact that they feature in some of the best-known quotations of all time suggests that they are peculiarly susceptible to being noticed, reported and remembered. But before the aspiring contemporary political orator can make it into a dictionary of quotations, there are two more immediate hurdles to be crossed. First he must say something which impresses the audience to whom he is speaking. And second, news of what he has said must be picked up and reported in the media. Reaching this second stage is, of course, much easier said than done. Even if the press, radio and television take the trouble to be present when a speech is being made, politicians face stiff competition for the limited space and time available for covering all the news on any particular day. What they say must therefore be impressive enough to be noticed not just by the reporters who actually attend, but by the editors and producers who make the highly selective decisions as to what goes on to the front pages of newspapers and into peak-time broadcast news bulletins.

By looking at how speeches get reported, a basis emerges for an evolutionary hypothesis about the process whereby some sayings survive beyond their original context to become enshrined in the hearts and minds of the masses, and eventually in the dictionaries of quotations. Of the thousands of sentences delivered in speeches, only a minority strike enough of a chord to elicit an immediate display of audience approval; of these, only a minority are selected for quoting, reporting or relaying in the mass media; and only a minority of these will have such an impact as to be remembered over a longer period. Verbal formats which elicit applause thus get off to a strong start in the struggle for survival and, at each stage in the process, it is likely that more of them will survive to the next than is the case with messages formulated in other ways.

Selection by newspapers

It was seen in the previous chapter that the *Time* magazine report on Ronald Reagan's speech accepting the Republican Party nomination as presidential candidate commented extensively on the audience response to it. In the following extract from the *New York Times* report on John F. Kennedy's acceptance speech at the Democratic Party convention in 1960, the author of the article actually reports the number of times the audience applauded during the course of the speech. And before that comment is reached, it will be noted that a considerable number of contrastive statements were selected for inclusion in the opening paragraphs of the report. It is also of interest that Kennedy depicted his overall programme as the *third* in a historical sequence of *three* great Democratic traditions: Woodrow Wilson's 'New Freedom', Franklin Roosevelt's 'New Deal' and his own 'New Frontier'.

> *Los Angeles, July 15* – Senator John F. Kennedy formally opened his Democratic Presidential campaign tonight with a warning that the national road to a 'New Frontier' called for more sacrifices, not more luxuries.
>
> He slashed at his probable Republican Presidential rival,

Vice President Nixon, as he joined with his surprise Vice Presidential running mate, Senator Lyndon B. Johnson of Texas, in formally accepting nomination at the final session of the Democratic National Convention.

The 43 year old Massachusetts Senator said that world and domestic challenges required new positive answers to the unknown problems ahead. It is essential, he said, for Democrats to move beyond the New Deal and Fair Deal concepts.

CHALLENGES, NOT PROMISES

'Woodrow Wilson's New Freedom promised our nation a new political and economic framework,' Senator Kennedy said. 'Franklin Roosevelt's New Deal promised security and succor to those in need. But the New Frontier of which I speak is not a set of promises – it is a set of challenges.

'It sums up not what I intend to offer to the American people, but what I intend to ask of them. It appeals to their pride, it appeals to our pride, not our security – it holds out the promise of more sacrifice instead of more security.

'The New Frontier is here, whether we seek it or not.

'It would be easier to shrink from that frontier, to look to the safe mediocrity of the past, to be lulled with good intention and high rhetoric – and those who prefer that course should not vote for me or the Democratic party.'

Senator Kennedy was interrupted by applause thirty six times during his speech. (*New York Times*, 16 July 1960)

More recently, the punch line contained in the second part of a contrast used by Mrs Thatcher – 'You turn if you want to; the lady's not for turning' – made the headlines in all the British national newspapers. Most of the reports, as in plate 5.1, commented on the favourable audience responses to the speech, and inspection of the video tape reveals that the audience in fact applauded after each part of the contrast (for twelve and ten seconds respectively). The punch line of the contrast subsequently became sufficiently well known and well remembered for the mass circulation *Daily Mirror* to hark back to it in a front-page headline on Mrs Thatcher's reaction to a speech at the following year's conference (see plate 5.1).

Saturday, October 11, 1980   12p   TODAY'S SPORT STARTS ON PAGE 26

Maggie Coles . . . vendetta

POLICE CHIEF AND THE RADIO GIRL'S KNICKERS

By SUN REPORTER

A SCOTLAND YARD inspector allegedly told a radio reporter in the middle of a broadcast: "I am going to pull your knickers down and smack you."

It was part of a vendetta waged by Yard men against 29-year-old Maggie Coles, an industrial tribunal heard yesterday.

Another officer put a dead mouse in her chair, it was claimed.

Finally, the tribunal was told, the hate campaign brought a furious outburst from Miss Coles, a London Broadcasting Company traffic reporter at the Yard.

Escorted

After being cut off during a broadcast, she burst into the Press office and launched a tirade of abuse.

She called Press officer Sandra Henney "a silly cow," the tribunal heard.

Eventually, she was escorted out by a policeman after twice refusing to leave.

Miss Coles was later sacked by LBC and is claiming unfair dismissal. She alleged that control room staff whistled and sang while she was on the air, tampered with her broadcasting equipment, and

— Continued on Page Two.

THE LADY'S NOT FOR TURNING!

NOW FOR A WINTER OF COMMON SENSE !
—Page 2

BATTLE RAGES AT BRIGHTON
—Pages 4, 5

Fight goes on, pledges Maggie

Triumph . . . Mrs Thatcher acknowledges her oration at the conference yesterday

■ PREMIER Maggie Thatcher yesterday gave her defiant answer to critics clamouring for a U-turn in Government policy . . . "You turn if you want to: The Lady's NOT for turning."

■ Delegates at the Tory conference in Brighton roared their approval as Maggie made a rallying call for "unity and common sense" as the Government entered its most difficult period.

■ She DEFENDED the Tories against accusations of callousness — "There is no other policy for solving our problems."

■ She WARNED of the Left-wing threat within the Labour Party— "Let their Orwellian nightmare be a spur for us to rebuild the fortunes of this free nation. If we fail that freedom could be imperilled."

■ And she PLEDGED the Government to solving the "human tragedy" of the two million jobless.

■ But while delegates rose to acclaim their leader, Left-wing rioters were causing chaos. Demonstrators sneaked into the hall as Mrs Thatcher was addressing the delegates —and hurled abuse. Outside they attacked police and threw flour bombs.

5.1   The second part of a contrast hits the headlines and is recalled a year later.

DAILY Mirror

Thursday, October 15, 1981   14p   ★★★

Mrs Di Smith flies out

By MIRROR REPORTER

HERE'S the one and only, unmistakable Princess of Wales pretending to be somebody completely different. She flew from London to Aberdeen last night with her detective, Inspecter Graham Smith. And in the hope that they would go unnoticed at Heathrow airport, the pair were listed as Mr. and Mrs. Smith, but Diana, eye-catching as ever in a cream outfit with a peach blouse, found that the trick had failed. Photographers were waiting. And eventually, she gave them a rueful smile.

● The Princess is to switch on London's Christmas Illuminations in Regent Street on November 18.

Picture by: VICTOR CRAWSHAW

The one picture that says it all

TED HEATH'S attempt to secure a Blackpool beachhead in his fight against Thatcherism was beaten back yesterday.

Yet he has not lost the war.

It is true that by mid-afternoon he had been routed in the Tory conference. But as dusk fell, Sir Ian Gilmour, his ally, launched an even more vicious counterattack against the Government.

It was an extraordinary day even by the standards of British political-conference-scene.

Never before, not even in the aftermath of Suez or during the leadership battle of 1963, has the Tory Party been so divided, so abusive, so full of personal hatred and so like the Labour Party.

Mrs Thatcher looked resigned, bored even, during Mr Heath's speech, not listening to his message.

Booed

But she must remember—and if she doesn't I will remind her—that at last year's conference she said:

"This week has demonstrated that we are a party united in purpose, strategy and resolve—and we actually like each other."

What a difference a year makes.

Yesterday's events included:

● Ted Heath being booed, hissed and slow-handclapped in the Blackpool arena where he used to receive five-minute standing ovations when he was Prime Minister.

● Chancellor Sir Geoffrey Howe declaring doggedly that despite every criticism government policy would be unchanged—and having a bash at Mr. Heath in the process.

● Former Cabinet Minister Sir Ian Gilmour maintaining that unless we said goodbye to Mrs. Thatcher's strategy we could say goodbye to the British economy.

Sir Ian, a member of Mrs. Thatcher's Cabinet only a month ago, was withering about

TURN-OFF: Mrs. Thatcher rests her eyes during Ted Heath's speech.   Picture: BILL ROWNTREE

THE LADY'S NOT FOR LISTENING

By TERENCE LANCASTER
Mirror Political Editor

her when he spoke at an evening fringe meeting on the Government's record.

Output was down, he said, bankruptcies and closures were up and unemployment had more than doubled.

"Most of this happened in the attempt to slay the dragon of inflation," said Sir Ian. "But the dragon is still more bloated than it was at the last election."

Government policies had actually worsened and put up prices as well.

But if Sir Ian was winning the argument outside the conference hall, the conference itself rejected Mr. Heath wholeheartedly.

His speech was brave, but appeared to sway nobody, though on the platform Willie Whitelaw and Francis Pym, two well-known wets, appeared to agree with every word of it.

Mr. Heath's eight minutes on the rostrum

was a daring attempt to get the party to endorse mild inflation and break out from the vicious circle of international interest rates.

But the boos started even before he did.

And speaker after speaker attacked him.

A councillor from Stockton said that while the two past and present leaders had visions, "Mrs Thatcher has a vision that one day Britain will be great again and Ted Heath has a vision that

● Turn to Page Two

135

Mr Benn's 'Thousand peers' speech, which was discussed in the previous chapter, also dominated the next day's newspaper headlines. The front page of the *Guardian* carried a picture of him taking a photograph of Mr Healey, and the headline for the report on the whole of the previous day's proceedings at the conference refers directly to Mr Benn's speech. The opening paragraph then takes it as the starting-point, and notes that it was 'received with rapture'. Lower down in the report, Mr Benn's performance is compared favourably with that of Mr Healey, and is depicted as the climax to an otherwise 'lacklustre' debate. The proposal to abolish the House of Lords by creating a thousand peers is then singled out as the 'most popular' part of his programme, and is also the first proposal to be singled out for a mention.

It will be remembered that in Mr Benn's proposal to abolish the House of Lords the audience started to applaud in anticipation of what he was about to say (see extract 44, page 101), and this was probably one of the factors which resulted in its being singled out as the most popular. The applause also went on for twenty seconds, which is far in excess of the eight-second norm. This in turn may well have had something to do with the fact that the 'thousand peers' proposal was not just the *third* of *three* pieces of proposed legislation, but *contrasted* in form with the first two. As can be seen from the more detailed report from an inside page of the same day's *Guardian*, the abolition of the House of Lords was presented as a necessary procedural measure without which it would be impossible to get the first two Bills enacted (plate 5.3). In other words, the third proposal stood out in contrast with the first two in the same way as 'so few' contrasted with 'so much' and 'so many' in the famous Churchillian three-part list mentioned earlier.

These examples illustrate a more general observation about the excerpts from speeches which are most likely to become front-page news – messages packaged as contrasts and three-part lists are frequently featured in prominent positions in headlines and news reports, especially when they were greeted at the time by a longer than usual burst of applause. It can thus be seen that audience responses are extremely important when it comes to assessing the relative impact of different politicians and policy proposals, and that they have a direct bearing on who and what is deemed worthy of front-page coverage. Journalists obviously do not go as far as to carry around 'clapometers' of the sort sometimes used to decide winners in quizzes and talent-spotting competitions. But they do monitor the frequency and duration of applause and use the results as a kind of informal barometer for measuring the effectiveness or otherwise of speeches as a whole, and of particular passages from them. And it is not at all clear that there are any other similarly tangible measures that could be relied on for making such assessments.

Selection by broadcasters

Messages which elicit an audience response have additional attractions for the producers of radio and television news programmes. The severe time constraints within which they work mean that they cannot hope to replay as many verbatim passages from a speech as can be quoted in a newspaper report. The standard solution to this problem involves picking out 'choice extracts' to accompany and illustrate the report on any particular speech. In the selection, sequences which get applauded have two main advantages over and above the fact that the applause helps to identify points which attracted the immediate attention and approval of the audience being addressed. One is that such messages tend to come in a very *brief* package, which means that they do not take up too big a slice of the limited time available for the news bulletin as a whole. The other advantage is that the statements are *complete* in themselves, which makes the job of editing the tape very much easier – just as audiences treat completion points as places to start clapping, so too do news editors treat them as convenient natural boundaries, where taped extracts can be cut without it appearing to viewers or listeners that the flow of a speaker's argument was too abruptly interrupted.

A number of the excerpts discussed in earlier chapters were in fact examples of 'choice extracts' which had been selected for inclusion in broadcast news programmes. One of these was George Wallace's 'I say segregation now, segregation tomorrow, and segregation for ever' (extract 33, page 60), which was one

THE GUARDIAN

Printed in London and Manchester   Tuesday September 30 1980   18p

ANYTHING YOU CAN DO : Denis Healey, himself a well-known amateur photographer, poses at Blackpool for Tony Benn his rival for the Labour Party leadership. Picture by Don McPhee

Benn lays down laws for Labour

By Keith Harper,
Labour Editor

Mr Tony Benn's personal parliamentary programme for the first month of a new Labour Government was received with rapture at the start of the Labour Party conference yesterday, and all divisions were kept at bay in a serious attempt to present the party as a contender for office.

It was not a complete success because the party demonstrated that it was still at loggerheads over its approach to pay policy. But it gave two important contenders for Mr Callaghan's job, Mr Benn and Mr Denis Healey, the opportunity to display their worth and, as far as conference was concerned Mr Benn indisputably came off the better.

He delivered his own Queen's Speech at the end of a lacklustre debate on the economy by setting out his three immediate pieces of legislation for the next Labour Government as if it were his own personal election address. The most popular of these proved to be the abolition of the House of Lords by the creation of a thousand new Labour peers at the time the Bill went through to make sure that the task was carried out.

That might take a month, he thought. But his other reforms might take weeks, even days. The first was a short, sharp Industry Bill to give the government powers to carry out further nationalisation and to introduce industrial democracy, and the second an Act which would give to the House or Commons the power that had been taken away from it by the Common Market.

Mr Benn, like Mr Healey and Mr Michael Foot before him, went out of his way to stress the need for the party to unite against a Government which would leave Labour with the legacy of a "broken-backed economy with devastated areas." He allowed himself a brief dalliance with incomes policy to the extent of saying that it was not possible to have wage restraint while profits and investment were allowed to run free.

Mr Benn was given a royal reception. In contrast. Mr Healey was hissed long and loudly as he made his way to the rostrum for his four-minute offering. He forecast 3 million unemployed by this time next year and accused Mrs Thatcher of dragging the "red hot rake of unemployment through the West Mid-

Leader comment, page 10 ; Conference reports, page 4 ; Peter Jenkins commentary, page 15 : Gang of Three fight back and Sketch, back page

lands, and even the lush green pastures of the South-east.

Mr Healey unashamedly put down his marker as a price and incomes man but made it clear that the party would stand no chance of removing Mrs Thatcher from office if it kept fighting itself. For Mr Healey it was not an aggressive speech, but he did emphasise that Labour had to provide the leadership for which the nation was crying out.

Mr Foot's contribution should have been devoted to a review of Labour's plan to revitalise industry, but it dealt mainly "on the home-made British catastrophe directed from Downing Street." Mr Foot was daring enough to suggest that Mrs Thatcher's Government would not last the course, a view not generally held in Blackpool, at least by union leaders.

He elicited little response to his suggestion that the next Labour Government would have to mobilise Britain's resources on a scale never achieved in peacetime, but won much sympathy for his proposition that this week "we must restore and rally our friends, and confound our enemies." Labour's role, he believed, was to serve and save the people

In spite of the undoubted attempts to show the world that Labour was not at odds with itself and in reasonable shape to get Mrs Thatcher out

Turn to back page, col. 5

5.2   Mr Benn monopolizes the headlines above the coverage of the previous day's party conference proceedings.

5.3 (right)   From the more detailed coverage on an inside page, it emerges that the most popular proposal was the third of three.

Benn calls for end of the Lords and more nationalisation

Mr Tony Benn, winding up the debate on the economy and replying on behalf of the NEC, spelled out three measures Labour should carry out as soon as it returned to power. The first was an Industry Bill, which would give powers to extend common ownership, and to control capital movements, to provide for industrial democracy. That Bill, he said, must be on the statute book within days of Labour taking over.

The second piece of legislation must transfer power back from the European Economic Community to the House of Commons. The third would be to abolish the House of Lords, since the first two would not get through the Lords.

This would have to be done by electing 1,000 peers (presu-

party should begin at this conference by recommitting itself to full employment, expanded public services, and self-management, as an alternative to market forces and "hideous" bureaucracy.

Enormous damage was being done by the Government, not just by Mrs Thatcher, that was destroying major industry, affecting women, damaging ethnic communities and cutting education, health, and social services. Labour would inherit the broken-backed economy. Labour, he concluded, must support the idea of workers' initiatives, something recognised especially in Scotland, Wales, and Merseyside.

Mr Terry Duffy, the new AUEW leader, spoke of TUC efforts in trying to get the Gov-

ECONOMIC DEBATE.... 3

mably Labour) and abolishing peerages at the time that Bill went through. After terrific cheers, he added : "It is not possible to continue if it (a Labour Government) has control over only half a Parliament."

Finally, Mr Benn added, the party must stand up to the pressures these policies would bring about—"The pressures of the IMF, by the EEC, and the bullyboys in the City of London, who would test us within hours as to whether we are serious."

He believed it was a democratic, socialist, and moderate programme, compared to the magnitude of the task the party would face.

Mr Benn further believed that a campaign for this policy would unite the people and give the party the majority it needed to carry the programme through if it was pursued with courage and clarity.

It was appropriate that the

ernment to take action over unemployment — "the biggest cancer in our midst." The TUC was trying to persuade the Government to ease the burden by selective import controls, but it was two months before the Prime Minister would meet the TUC, and it did not expect her to be receptive.

Meanwhile, something had to be done about the Japanese, who were now intending to infiltrate the heavy vehicle industry, he said. Britain's competitors had government assistance, which was not available here.

The TUC was further asking the Government to ease the tremendous costs of energy, so that industry could be more competitive. What, he asked, was wrong with the Government pioneering a reduction in working hours ? It was necessary to steer the number of man-hours available wherever possible, to relieve unemployment.

of two passages featured in an Independent Television News report on his 1982 campaign for the governorship of Alabama. The other choice extract was a contrast, in which a puzzling first part was resolved by an insulting punch line aimed at the Federal government in Washington. The audience responded as soon as the second part of the contrast was completed, and Wallace's additional clause was therefore almost drowned out by the applause.

---

(71) (Alabama state governorship campaign, 1982)

Wallace: Ⓐ→ Being paralysed in the legs is nothing.
(0.3)

Ⓑ→ { The trouble with our country in this last ten or twenty or thirty years has been that we've had too many people in Washington para-lysed in the
head ⌐instead of being in the leg.

Audience: └x-xxXXXXXXXXXXXXXXXXXX ....

It is much more usual for only one extract to be selected for replaying on broadcast news programmes, even in the case of major speeches like presidential inaugurals. When François Mitterrand was officially installed as president of France, for example, BBC Television's *Newsnight* chose a single passage from his inaugural address as being worthy of translating and quoting verbatim to British viewers. As film of President Mitterrand making the speech was shown on screen, the commentary went as follows:

---

(72) (*Newsnight*, BBC Television, May 1981)

Voiceover: 'My intention,' said President Mitterrand in his inaugural address, 'is to convince and not to conquer.'

In the original French, this simple contrast would presumably have had a more poetic ring to it ('*à convaincre et pas à vaincre*'), a fact which may have made it all the more noticeable to those who decided to select it for relaying to the British audience.

A few months earlier, Ronald Reagan had taken office as president of the United States, and a sixty-minute early-evening news programme (*P.M.*, BBC Radio 4) selected another single extract to be replayed from his inaugural address. In this case, the fact that the choice had been based on an assessment of the audience responses was made quite clear in the introduction to it – listeners were informed that this was the passage for which President Reagan had received the longest burst of applause. Inspection of the full recording of the speech shows that the clapping went on for three seconds longer than the usual eight seconds. It also shows that the boastful message about American attitudes towards peace was packaged by means of the relatively rare combined verbal format in which the third item in a three-part list contrasts with the first two. Completion is then finally reached with a further brief contrast between the present and the future.

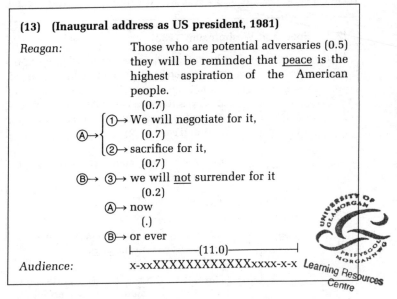

One year later, President Reagan made another historic speech, when he became the first American president ever to address the members of both Houses of Parliament at Westminster. The BBC Television programme *Newsnight* again showed

141

only a single excerpt in its report on the event. In the introduction to it, the commentary referred to the passage as the only one from the entire speech which the audience applauded. The possible significance of this even became a matter for discussion immediately afterwards in a studio interview with former prime minister Edward Heath – the issue being whether the audience had considered the occasion to be too ceremonial for much applause to be appropriate, or whether more than just this one burst of applause might have been reasonably expected.

In any event, the message was designed, packaged and delivered so effectively that it is not at all surprising that the audience did in fact applaud. In common with the memorable speeches referred to at the end of the last chapter, it is an excellent example of a speaker saying just the right thing at just the right time and in just the right place. He thus praised the principles at stake in the Falklands campaign, at a time when

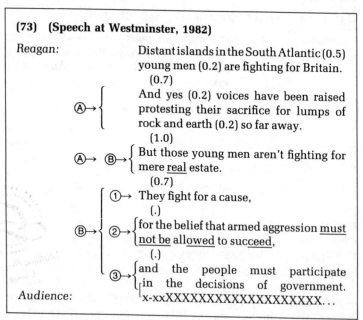

(73)   (Speech at Westminster, 1982)

Reagan:
Distant islands in the South Atlantic (0.5) young men (0.2) are fighting for Britain.
(0.7)

Ⓐ→ And yes (0.2) voices have been raised protesting their sacrifice for lumps of rock and earth (0.2) so far away.
(1.0)

Ⓐ→ Ⓑ→ But those young men aren't fighting for mere <u>real</u> estate.
(0.7)

Ⓑ→
①→ They fight for a cause,
(.)
②→ for the belief that armed aggression <u>must not be</u> all<u>owed</u> to suc<u>ceed</u>,
(.)
③→ and the people must participate in the decisions of government.

Audience: x-xxXXXXXXXXXXXXXXXXXX...

military action was in progress, and did so in front of the very people who had taken the decision to send the British task force to the South Atlantic. The way the message was packaged was also technically very impressive, involving as it does a very unusual combination of interlocking devices: the second part of a first contrast doubles as the first part of a further contrast, the second part of which is a three-part list. It is therefore hardly surprising that the audience started to applaud very soon after the 'and' had projected that the third item would be the last, and that the picture being broadcast to viewers could be switched from President Reagan to his wife and Mrs Thatcher in time for them to be seen moving their hands apart in readiness to start clapping.

Selection during an election

If excerpts featuring the verbal formats which regularly elicit applause are also the ones most likely to be selected for replaying in broadcasts, it is instructive to consider what happens during an election campaign, when politicians are competing to make the most of the air time available to them. It will thus be important for politicians and parties to generate a continual supply of quotable quotes that the media will be able to pick up and disseminate to the electorate.

Before considering what these were in the British election campaign in 1983, it should be noted that, for reasons to be considered further in the next chapter, the advent of mass television has brought about a marked decline in the importance of traditional oratory during election campaigns. This is reflected by the fact that Mrs Thatcher only made six set-piece speeches in the course of the 1983 campaign. There was also a great reduction in the amount of televised coverage of speeches, which preliminary research suggests may have been by as much as 80 per cent between the 1979 and 1983 elections. One problem, of course, is that major speeches tend to be made in the evenings, which makes the inclusion of excerpts almost impossible for early-evening news bulletins, and difficult for mid-evening programmes. And by the next evening, last night's speeches seldom qualify as today's news. None the less, a few minutes worth of excerpts from speeches were broadcast on

143

most mid-evening news programmes during the campaign, and a comparison of the performances of the Conservative and Labour leaders reveals some interesting differences.

Both parties started the campaign on fairly equal terms as far as the formats of their election slogans were concerned. The Conservatives fielded a contrast, 'Britain's on the right track. Don't turn back', with Labour fighting under the three-part list 'Think positive, act positive, vote Labour'. However, Mrs Thatcher showed much greater ability than Mr Foot to produce statements that could be readily quoted or replayed on television. For her major speeches, she used the sincerity machine, which meant that viewers saw a confident-looking leader apparently speaking without a script. Right at the beginning of the campaign, Independent Television News screened an excerpt in which two points formulated as contrasts were applauded by the audience:

---

(37) (UK general election, 1983)

Thatcher: Which example will be most likely to make it
             pause?
                (0.7)

Ⓐ→ { The renunciation of the means of national
      self defence (0.4) which the banners of Fas-
      laine and Greenham call for
                (0.7)

Ⓑ→ { or the swift and sure response of our young
      men in the South Atlantic just a year ago.
             |————————(8.0)————————|

Audience: x-xxXXXXXXXXXXXXXXXXXX
Thatcher: ... this is a historic election (1.0) for the
             choice facing the nation (0.5) is between two
             totally different ways of life.
                (1.0)
             And what a prize we have to fight for.
                (1.0)

Ⓐ→ { No less than the chance to banish from our
      land (0.4) the dark divisive clouds of marxist
      socialism
                (0.7)

> and to bring together men and women from all walks of life (0.7) who share a belief in freedom (0.4) and who have the courage to uphold it.
>
> Ⓑ→
>
> *Audience:* x-xxXXXXX (TV editor's cut)

Later in that first week, the following combined format was featured in an excerpt shown on BBC Television's *Nine o'clock News:*

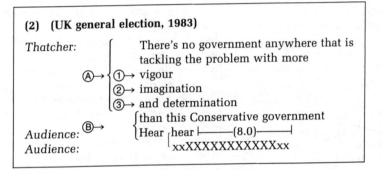

(2)   (UK general election, 1983)

Thatcher: There's no government anywhere that is tackling the problem with more
Ⓐ→ ①→ vigour
②→ imagination
③→ and determination
than this Conservative government
Ⓑ→
Audience: Hear ⌈hear ⊢————(8.0)————⌉
Audience: xxXXXXXXXXXXXXxx

On the day that the Tory manifesto was published, BBC's *Early Evening News* headlines singled out a striking three-part list from Mrs Thatcher's briefing speech to Conservative candidates, a quotation which was repeated at the end of the bulletin and on *all* subsequent news broadcasts that evening:

(74)   (UK general election, 1983)

Newsreader: The Conservatives launch their election manifesto and Mrs Thatcher tells candidates to remain cool, calm and ~~elected~~.

In the main reportage which followed later in the programme, the newsreader's summary of the manifesto itself was partially formulated in terms of contrasts and a three-part list:

(75)   (UK general election, 1983)

Newsreader:

The Conservatives have launched their Manifesto setting out their plans for what they hope will be their second term of office.

Mrs Thatcher, in a foreword to the document, says that the choice before the nation is stark:

(A)→ { either to continue progress towards recovery,

(B)→ { (A)→ { or to follow policies more extreme and damaging

(B)→ { than those ever put forward by any previous opposition.

Senior Ministers went to the Conservative Central Office to help Mrs Thatcher present their Manifesto. In it they acknowledge they face three main challenges:

①→ Defence of the country,

②→ employment of the people,

③→ and prosperity of the economy.

Our chief political correspondent Brian Curtois analyses the document....

Later in the same news broadcast, when coverage turned to the actual press conference, what Mrs Thatcher herself said was introduced with a three-part list and a contrast:

(76)   (UK general election, 1983)

Thatcher:

①→ { The Manifesto I believe you will find a robust work.

②→ { It contains proposals which are both sound and adventurous

③→ { and is designed to meet the challenge of our times.

(A)→ { Some of the policies in it represent the continuity factor in politics

(B)→ and others the need for change.

on notes or a script, but in the 1983 election he was seen in most of the excerpts shown on television news programmes to be almost totally tied to his text. This was evidently a party decision in response to complaints by journalists about his tendency to depart too far from press releases containing prepared scripts. Consequently, in the absence of a teleprompter like the one used by Mrs Thatcher, and not possessed of exceptional eyesight, Mr Foot regularly appeared as a hunched figure, glued to the lectern, and seldom able to raise his head from a script he was finding difficult to read.

If the excerpts actually televised are anything to go by, either he or his script-writers showed little capacity to deploy the sorts of verbal format most likely to elicit applause. Indeed, observations made so far have failed to yield a single excerpt shown on early or mid-evening BBC news programmes in which there was so much as a single burst of applause. Nor have any instances been noted to date of quotes in which something is formulated in terms of a contrast or three-part list. More usually, what he said had to be paraphrased by news reporters with phrases like 'Today Mr Foot talked about...', rather than 'Mr Foot said....' This is of course wholly consistent with the suggestion that he was not nearly as effective as Mrs Thatcher in producing directly quotable quotes. At the same time, the absence of effectively deployed applause-elicitation devices also made it much more difficult for the producers of television news programmes to select and edit suitable excerpts from his speeches.

One of the consequences of the relative absence of applause during televised excerpts from Mr Foot's election speeches was that the mass audience saw little evidence that what he was saying was being warmly received even by the Labour faithful attending his meetings. At times, it almost appeared as if Mr Foot himself was becoming bored with the text he was reading. Thus, in the following example, which was broadcast immediately after an excerpt in which Mrs Thatcher had received several bursts of applause (extract 37), he showed signs of tiring while reciting a list of six rhetorical questions. And, in contrast with the earlier mentioned series of such questions by Neil Kinnock (extract 6), there is no appropriately formulated answer of the sort which could have produced an instant burst of applause. The opportunity to capitalize on any cumulative impact this series of questions might have had is thus lost without a suitably formulated answer or summary statement to prompt applause.

---

(78)   (UK general election, 1983)

Foot: ... who would have voted for them (0.8) if they had known that they would have destroyed more jobs than the previous (0.2) eight governments together have created?
    (1.0)
Who would have voted for them if they had known (0.4) that they would reduce our manufacturing output to four fifths (0.4) of its previous (0.2) level?
    (0.8)
Who would have voted for them if they had known that they would more than double rents and raise the mortgage rate by nearly (0.2) a half?
    (0.8)
Who would have (0.2) voted for them if they had known that they would nearly (0.2) double VAT within days and more than double (0.2) inflation within a year?
    (0.2)
Who would have voted for them if they had known (0.2) that the crime rate would rise (0.4) by a third?
    (.)
Who would have voted for them if they had known that they would increase prescription charges by six hundred per cent from (.) twenty pence to one pound forty?
    (1.0)
If Labour had (.) stayed in office (1.0) the oil shock (0.8) which so afflicted other industrial countries would have passed us by because we were (0.4) rapidly approaching self-sufficiency (0.2) in oil. (0.8) As the only (0.4) major industrial country self-sufficient in oil (0.2) we could have become (.) one of the most prosperous nations in the world during this period....

Extract (79) below comes from another excerpt which was broadcast immediately after one from a speech by Mrs Thatcher which had been punctuated by applause (extract 2). Here again, the mass television audience was exposed to yet another long sequence of talk being received in total silence:

---

(79) (UK general election, 1983)

Foot: ... Thatcher (0.5) Tebbit Toryism contemplates with complacency (0.7) the continuance of three and three quarter million unemployed (0.8) more than a million of them under twenty five (1.0) and more than a million of them unemployed for (.) more than a year (0.7) and they contemplate that for (0.4) year after year after (0.4) year ahead it has no comprehension (1.0) Thatcher Tebbit Toryism has no comprehension or concern (0.5) how deep will be the divisions and injustices (0.5) thereby enforced on our society (0.7). It sets no date (1.0) when these horrific figures will start to fall and dares to talk of (0.3) national recovery (0.5) while these figures (0.4) still rise. ...

Closer inspection of the transcripts of these excerpts from Mr Foot's speeches reveals that they do in fact contain a number of contrastive and three-parted elements. Live audiences, however, only hear the words once, and are thus unable to identify and respond to formats unless the speaker takes care to deliver them in such a way as to make it clear what they are. A serious technical weakness in Mr Foot's oratory during the 1983 election appears to have been that his timing, intonation and non-verbal behaviour did not directly assist audiences to recognize when they should applaud. And this apparent inability to project identifiable completion points is almost certainly one of the factors which have resulted in Mr Foot's reputation as a 'rambling' speaker.

On the basis of research done so far, it appears that what television viewers saw of speeches performed by Mrs Thatcher and Mr Foot is likely to have left them with very different impressions of the two main party leaders. Mrs Thatcher was regularly seen speaking confidently 'without a script', and to be saying things which her audiences approved of strongly enough to respond with whole-hearted bursts of applause. Such excerpts were then frequently followed by ones showing Mr Foot having difficulty in reading from a prepared text, and saying things which were almost invariably received in total silence. Even viewers who paid no attention whatsoever to what either of them was actually saying would thus be likely to be more impressed by Mrs Thatcher's performances than those by Mr Foot. And as far as those who did listen were concerned, they were supplied with many more potentially noticeable, memorable and quotable quotes by Mrs Thatcher than by Mr Foot.

Selection by other persuaders

The various examples included above suggest that the art of being quoted depends in the first place on saying something which has an immediate impact on the audience to whom it is actually addressed. Because such a high proportion of bursts of applause occur after contrasts and three-part lists, it is easy to see why messages packaged in this way are so regularly reproduced and replayed in the media, and why some of them survive much longer to become memorable quotations. There is some preliminary evidence to suggest that the combined use of verbal formats may be particularly effective, in that they tend to elicit responses which last for longer than the average eight seconds, and hence stand a better chance of being noticed and reported by the press, radio and television.

Contrasts and three-part lists are widely used not just by political orators and their speech-writers. They are also regularly found in other spoken and written materials where the aim is to persuade an audience. They are, for example, much favoured by advertising copywriters as a means of formulating slogans, and a collection of examples can be readily accumulated during an evening's television viewing or by glancing through the pages of almost any newspaper or magazine.

Contrasts and three-part lists also tend to come thick and fast in more extended texts written with a view to eliciting the approval of readers. In newspapers, for example, the most explicitly 'persuasive' sections are the editorials, and it is here that these verbal formats are most often found. Sometimes, as in

Table 5.1 Advertising slogans

	slogan	product and source
A	The sort of elegance you can remember.	Jacket
B	The sort of price you'd forgotten.	(Sunday colour supplement)
A	Lazy evenings,	Housecoat
B	busy mornings.	(Sunday colour supplement)
A	Heavy 100% silk shirts at	Shirts
B	very light prices.	(Sunday colour supplement)
A	See the Left Bank	Holidays in Paris
B	at the Right Price.	(British Rail poster)
A	Great big mountains,	Holidays in Wales
B	great little trains.	(Radio Times)
A	Times change	Cognac
B	but Martell never varies.	(Sunday colour supplement)
A	Now you can afford to be out	Telephone answering
B	when the call comes in.	machines (Sunday colour supplement)
1	A paint,	Shop's own-brand paint
2	a store,	(US TV commercial)
3	a whole lot more.	
	All you need	
1	to dust,	Furniture polish
2	clean	(US TV commercial)
3	and polish.	
	A Mars a day helps you	
1	work,	Chocolate bar
2	rest,	(British TV commercial)
3	and play.	
1	Any time,	Vermouth
2	any place,	(British TV commercial)
3	anywhere.	

Mirror Comment

Paying the Con men

WHAT Britain needed from the Budget was Hope. What it got was another dose of Howe.

The slide to disaster not only goes on. It accelerates. The Chancellor doesn't understand where he has gone wrong and so he does more of the same.

More people will be out of work after this Budget, not fewer.

The standard of living of almost everyone — not just the smoker, the drinker and the motorist — will fall.

Where the Chancellor has given he has given meanly. Where he has taken, he has pillaged the pocket.

Pensioners are denied the full increase to which they are entitled. Lower paid workers, in particular, are being robbed of the tax relief which should be automatic.

The party which promised to tax **LESS** is taxing **MORE**. It promised to spend **LESS** and it is spending **MORE**. It promised to borrow **LESS**, yet it is borrowing **MORE**.

The road to the next election will be paved with its broken promises.

There is small help for small businesses. But precious little for the big firms, the big employers.

Can Mrs. Thatcher or Sir Geoffrey understand the feelings of the men and women in the street this morning?

Council rents are rising by £3 or £4 or more a week. Cigarettes, a pint and the cost of running a car all go up.

The increase in petrol alone will affect the price of almost everything sold in the shops.

Once again, the heaviest burdens fall upon those least able to bear them.

The Budget smashes the most solemn promises by which the Government tricked its way into power. It is not a prescription for future success. It is a repetition of past failure.

It means more inflation, more unemployment, more taxation and m o r e borrowing. It is the price the country must pay for ever believing the Con men.

5.4   Persuasive writing like this *Daily Mirror* editorial frequently involves the same verbal formats as those that elicit applause.

the editorial from the mass-circulation *Daily Mirror* shown in plate 5.4, they are made up almost exclusively of contrasts and three-part lists. This example also illustrates how typographical aids can be used to compensate for an author's inability to use intonation and non-verbal signals to give added emphasis. In certain places heavier type is used, and the key contrastive words in the triple contrast halfway down are made to stand out with capital letters.

In some respects, this editorial is reminiscent of the extract from the speech by Tony Benn, in which one contrast followed after another, each one prompting the audience to applaud (extract 45, pages 103–4). Similarly, had the editorial been a text for a speech, rather than for publication in a newspaper, it might well in its performance have been punctuated by frequent bursts of applause. And this may in fact provide an important clue as to why the writers of persuasive texts so frequently employ the verbal devices that most regularly elicit applause. For it suggests that the art of this kind of writing lies in packaging messages in such a way that the readers will 'silently applaud' at regular intervals in the course of reading a text: just as contrasts and three-part lists strike chords in such a way as to prompt immediate displays of approval from members of an audience, so too may they be capable of having a similar impact on readers.

With this possibility in mind, it is interesting to look at one of the most influential persuasive texts ever written, namely The *Communist Manifesto* by Marx and Engels. As can be seen from the following extract from its first section, an impressive number of contrasts are deployed in rapid succession:

---

(80)   (Karl Marx and Friedrich Engels, *The Manifesto of the Communist Party*, 1848)

BOURGEOIS AND PROLETARIANS

The history of all hitherto existing society is the history of class struggles.

Freeman and slave, patrician and plebeian, lord and serf, guildmaster and journeyman, in a word, oppressor and oppressed, stood in constant opposition to one another, carried on an uninterrupted, now hidden, now open fight, a fight that

---

each time ended, either in a revolutionary reconstruction of society at large, or in the common ruin of the contending classes.

In the earlier epochs of history, we find almost everywhere a complicated arrangement of society into various orders, a manifold gradation of social rank. In ancient Rome we have patricians, knights, plebeians, slaves; in the Middle Ages, feudal lords, vassals, guildmasters, journeymen, apprentices, serfs; in almost all of these classes, again, subordinate gradations.

The modern bourgeois society that has sprouted from the ruins of feudal society has not done away with class antagonisms. It has but established new classes, new conditions of oppression, new forms of struggle in place of the old ones.

Our epoch, the epoch of the bourgeoisie, possesses, however, this distinctive feature: It has simplified the class antagonisms. Society as a whole is more and more splitting up into two great hostile camps, into two great classes directly facing each other, bourgeoisie and proletariat.

It is not just that this particular passage includes a large number of contrasts, but it also presents the more general Marxist view of nineteenth-century society as being made up of only two *contrasting* classes, the bourgeoisie and the proletariat. The history of society is also divided into *three* main stages: an ancient period, the middle ages and 'our epoch'. Moreover, the *third* one is depicted as contrasting with the first two because of the simplification involved in the transition from situations where there was a 'manifold gradation of ranks' to one where there are only 'two great classes directly facing each other'. Such a view of history is, of course, perfectly consistent with the 'dialectic method' of analysis favoured by Marx and his followers. What is interesting, however, is that this method itself is based on a *three-stage* view of progress involving a 'thesis', 'antithesis' and 'synthesis', in which the first two phases contrast with each other, but are then reconciled in the third. The synthesis then becomes a new 'thesis', which will subsequently be opposed in the next period, and so on *ad infinitum*.

More generally, Marx's writings abound with interpretations of how society is supposed to work, almost all of which have two characteristics in common. One is that most of what he says can be read as criticisms or insults directed towards the capitalist *status quo*. And the other is that his messages are mainly expressed in terms of contrastive distinctions: *idealism–materialism, scientific–utopian* socialism, *base–superstructure, capital–labour, profits–wages, consciousness–false consciousness,* a class *in itself–for itself,* etc. In other words, the interpretations of society propagated by Marx are not only examples of a major type of applaudable message (i.e. criticisms or insults aimed at 'them'), but were packaged by means of the verbal format most regularly used to formulate such messages (i.e. the contrast). It may therefore be no coincidence that his work has struck so many chords with so many people for so many years.

To suggest this is to suggest a possible explanation of what Engels once referred to as 'the peculiar influence' of Marx's writings. By this he meant the extraordinary impact they had had, even within his lifetime, and their subsequent global consequences for national and international politics. Marx's 'peculiar influence' remains a puzzle a century later, and large numbers of intellectuals have spent a great deal of time trying to solve it. The most usual approach to the problem has been to look for reasons why the actual content of his theories have been so attractive to particular groups of people at particular times in particular regions of the world. The observations reported in this book point to a quite different approach to the problem of explaining Marx's enduring appeal. They suggest that his 'peculiar influence' may have had much to do with the types of message he was communicating and the verbal devices used in formulating and summarizing them. Throughout his work, Marx exhibited a remarkable and sustained ability to write in such a way that, had his texts been scripts for political speeches, his audiences would have had very many opportunities to applaud.

Such a view is supported by the fact that Marx is by no means the only famous philosopher or social theorist to have attracted the attention and approval of readers by means of contrasts or three-part lists. For example, central to classical Greek political theory was a classification of government in *three* types: democracy, oligarchy and tyranny. Rousseau, as was noted earlier, is still remembered for the famous contrast 'Man is born free and everywhere is in chains' (extract 63, page 129). Auguste Comte, the Frenchman who coined the word 'sociology', also made his name with a *three-stage* theory of history – the theological, metaphysical and positive. In Freudian theory there is the famous contrast between the *conscious* and the *unconscious* as well as a renowned three-part list: *id, ego* and *superego*. Many similar examples are also to be found in the writings of social and behavioural scientists who are not so well known to the general public, but who have none the less had a major impact within the academic world.

It is, of course, much more difficult to demonstrate convincingly that the use of contrasts and three-part lists by writers has a direct impact on a diffuse audience of readers than it is to show how effective they are when used by orators. This is for the obvious reason that reading is a silent activity: there are no bursts of applause, or even any near equivalents, that provide similarly concrete proof that a particular type of sentence prompts a favourable response. As a result, the best that can be done is to look at writings which are either produced with persuasive intent, or are known to have attracted a great deal of attention and approval from a large readership. And when things like advertising slogans, newspaper editorials, and the writings of Karl Marx and other influential social theorists are taken as specimens for examination, it emerges that they often make extensive use of exactly the same types of message and verbal format as those which are most likely to elicit collective displays of approval from live audiences.

The appeal of contrasts and lists

The suggestion that contrasts are particularly noticeable and memorable was implicit in the extract from a letter to *The Times* referred to earlier:

---

(50) **(Norman St John-Stevas, letter to *The Times*, 28 October 1981)**

I recall [Mrs Thatcher's] brilliant television broadcast of January 17, 1979, which was such an important contribution to

---

> our subsequent election victory, when she concluded with the moving words: 'We shall have to learn again to be one nation, or one day we shall be no nation.' Such an arresting antithesis has remained in my mind ever since....

Whether Mrs Thatcher's concluding contrast had the widespread impact that Mr St John-Stevas claimed is not only highly debatable, but would also be quite impossible to prove one way or the other. However, it did apparently have a profound impact on Mr St John-Stevas himself, who reports that he found it both arresting and memorable – so much so that it was still in his mind more than two and a half years later. This highlights a much more general question arising from the findings reported in this book, namely, what is it about contrasts and three-part lists that gives them their arresting and memorable quality?

It is impossible to find a definite answer to this from direct observation, for the obvious reason that there is no way of getting inside people's heads in order to discover what goes on there in response to different verbal formats. However, some of the observations already reported provide a number of hints as to why messages formulated as contrasts and three-part lists tend to have such a widespread and powerful appeal.

For example, in chapter 3, it was noted that an advantage shared by contrasts and lists was that, once hearers had recognized that one or other was being delivered, a clearly recognizable completion point could be anticipated, and this in turn requires an increased level of attentiveness on the part of the audience. Another observation was that it is much more difficult for audiences to recognize the completion point of contrasts that are too long and drawn out, which are therefore less likely to elicit applause. A major advantage of these particular verbal formats, then, is that they provide a way of formulating the gist of a message which is both brief and complete in itself. In fact, this point has been repeatedly illustrated throughout the book by the ease with which it has been possible to include short extracts which have been complete enough to be perfectly understandable *without* having to look at the whole speeches from which they were drawn. It has also been seen that editors of broadcast news programmes and dictionaries of quotations can confidently rely on people being able to grasp the gist of a message from the brief extracts they select. And that brevity has positive virtues as far as most people are concerned is confirmed by the general preference for short utterances in everyday conversational communication discussed in chapter 1.

In adversarial contexts, contrasts also provide an economical way of formulating rival positions. By distilling debatable issues into starkly contrasting alternatives, a politician can present his audiences with a summary of both sides of an argument, and do so in such a way that one will be instantly recognizable to them as being self-evidently preferable from 'our' point of view – and hence potentially worthy of a concrete display of approval.

Another 'arresting' feature of contrasts and three-part lists is that they provide a snappy way of summarizing and simplifying quite complicated arguments and ideas. As has been seen, contrasts often involve a puzzle-solution format, in which a common and highly effective technique for attracting attention (i.e. a puzzle) is used as a preliminary to supplying a clever punch line (the solution). Similarly, the sort of three-part list in which the third item contrasts with the first two also provides a concluding punch line like that featured in a multitude of three-part jokes. One standard format for these starts out with 'There was an Englishman, an Irishman and a Scotsman....' And the exclusion of a Welshman almost certainly has less to do with nationalistic prejudices than with the fact that such an addition would make a four-part joke, in which it would take longer to reach the contrastive punch line. Two preliminary segments are enough for hearers to be able to recognize a standard pattern and to appreciate any violation that occurs in the third segment. It is noticeable that children are familiarized with such a logic from a very early age by means of the multitude of three-part stories to which they are exposed – 'Goldilocks and the three bears', the 'Three little pigs', the 'Three Billy Goats gruff', etc. – where the fate of a third character contrasts sharply with that of the other two.

As was seen earlier, lists of three which can be heard as belonging to the same class of phenomena provide speakers with a way of underlining or giving progressively more emphasis to the point being made, and doing so in such a way as to give the impression that all possibilities have been covered and there is nothing else to be said on the matter (as in George Wallace's 'Segregation today, segregation tomorrow, and segregation for ever').

That three-part lists have an air of definite completeness about them is supported by the way speakers in ordinary conversation also routinely treat third items as utterance-completion points. It is worth reflecting on why this might be so. The most plausible explanation would seem to be that three is the minimum number required for it to be unambiguously clear that a list is indeed a list of similar items. Two consecutive items are enough to suggest that there is a link which establishes them as possible members of some more general class of phenomena, a possibility which is confirmed beyond doubt only when a third similar item is provided. Then, once the existence of a common thread has been firmly established, there is less to be gained by adding more and more items, in that the more a list is extended beyond the third one, the more redundant does each addition become. Three is therefore not just the *minimal* number necessary to eliminate any residual ambiguity there may be about the connection between a series of items; it is also the *maximally economical* number for doing this without labouring a point unduly. In other words, three parts are enough to permit a link to be identified unequivocally, without at the same time being too many to underline it excessively.

While contrasts and three-part lists provide a conveniently brief, snappy and apparently complete way of formulating messages, they supply people at the same time with 'food for thought': a certain amount of effort has to be put into the business of making sense of them. Although they are regularly used to convey boasts and insults, it is noticeable that speakers hardly ever explicitly announce that they are making an evaluative assertion about 'us' or 'them', even though this is what is in fact involved in the vast majority of applause-elicitation sequences. By deploying such verbal devices, they thus express messages indirectly rather than directly, and allow their audiences to 'see the point for themselves'. And this is arguably a critically important factor in accounting for their arresting and memorable quality.

A speaker who permits people to draw their own conclusions in effect shows greater respect for their intelligence and powers of reasoning than one who says something in such a direct and obvious way that only a fool could fail to see the point. If audiences feel they are being patronized or 'talked down to', they are unlikely to remain attentive, let alone be impressed by or remember what was said to them. More generally, there is a great deal of evidence from research into more everyday forms of communication to suggest that people not only routinely allow others latitude for arriving at their own interpretations of any particular utterance, but that there is a strong and very general preference for so doing. Obvious examples of the way messages tend to be expressed *indirectly* rather than directly are provided by the way we do things like making requests and issuing invitations. Formulations like 'Would you mind doing x?' are much more regularly used than the more direct 'Do x!' Similarly, invitations are typically preceded by preliminary enquiries like 'Are you doing anything tonight?', which are seldom if ever treated as neutral enquiries about our plans for the evening. Rather they are treated as an opportunity for prospective invitees to let it be known whether or not they will accept if an invitation is offered. Thus, we hardly ever approach someone and say, completely out of the blue, something like, 'I hereby invite you to dinner tonight.' The existence of a preference for the use of indirect versions of requests, invitations and many other routine activities, is shown not just by the fact that more direct formulations are much less frequently deployed, but also by the way in which the latter almost invariably sound at best excessively formal, and at worst abrupt or rude.

The sorts of difficulty politicians would run into if they formulated their messages more directly can perhaps best be judged by looking at paraphrases of famous contrasts and three-part lists. For example, it seems highly unlikely that 'I can't decide whether or not to commit suicide' would have achieved the same lasting impact as 'To be, or not to be'. This applies equally to most other famous quotations, as can be seen by comparing a selection of original indirect formulations with more direct ways of expressing the same sentiments:

(81)   (Paraphrases of some famous quotations)

indirect formulation	*direct formulation*
Ein Volk, ein Reich, ein Führer.	Germans are united in a nation-state under one leader.
Never in the field of human conflict has so much been owed by so many to so few.	The RAF pilots have done Britain the greatest possible service.
I have a dream that my four little children will one day live in a nation where they will not be judged by the colour of their skin, but by the content of their character.	I hope that racial discrimination in the United States of America will be abolished within a generation.
Two thousand years ago the proudest boast was 'Civis Romanus sum.' Today in the world of freedom, the proudest boast is 'Ich bin ein Berliner.'	Berlin is the symbol of a long-standing view of freedom.
You turn if you want to; the lady's not for turning.	No one will make me change my economic policies.
I counted them all out, and I counted them all back.	All the planes returned safely.

Such an exercise in paraphrase has the effect of translating formerly striking statements into versions which are so bland as to be totally unmemorable, even though the sense of each message is preserved. Unlike the originals, these more direct modes of communication leave nothing whatsoever to the imagination, and little or no effort is required to be able to see the point. The fact that this is so may well provide an important clue to understanding why messages formulated as contrasts or three-part lists are much more likely to be noticed and remembered than messages formulated in other ways. Anyone who has ever been tempted to consult books on how to acquire a superpower memory will know that the main piece of advice they offer is that one should learn to invent links between the items to be remembered, even (and especially) when no obvious link exists. By permitting or requiring listeners or readers to find the connections between the items in a list, or the parts of a contrast, speakers who deploy such verbal formats may well activate a similar process in the minds of their audiences. In order to identify and appreciate the point being made, people therefore have to put their brains to work. The increased mental effort involved in decoding interlocking contrasts and lists may consequently increase the chances that a particular message will remain in listeners' minds, especially if it comprises a suitably brief and punchy summary of a position with which they are already inclined to agree.

6   Televisuality

Television and the demise of live oratory

This book began with the observation that the success of many of the twentieth century's most influential political leaders was heavily dependent on their powers of oratory. After the 1960s, however, it becomes increasingly difficult to add new names to the list of politicians who have achieved widespread and unequivocal recognition as world-class orators. On a more local level, it is also noticeable that the careers of two of the most outstanding British orators of recent years, Enoch Powell and Tony Benn, have so far stopped short of the most glittering political prizes.

If we are witnessing a general decline in the importance of live oratory, a clue to why this might be so was offered by former prime minister Harold Macmillan during a televised interview shortly after the 1983 general election:

Although it may be something of an exaggeration to say that television has become so important that the art of public speaking is 'now almost gone', the view that television has become an increasingly dominant factor in contemporary political communication is one with which it would be foolish to disagree. So too must we accept that the art of performing effectively on television involves different skills to those which platform speakers have been able to rely on for more than 2000 years. The most obvious evidence for this is the fact that a screen actor with thirty years' experience of performing in front of film and television cameras has become president of the United States, since when there has been talk not just of elections by television, but of government by television. Equipped with the appropriate technical skills, it thus appears that a president can use televised addresses to the nation to mobilize voters to lobby their representatives so that they support presidential initiatives that might otherwise have failed to get through Congress. The extent of Ronald Reagan's success as a television communicator is further emphasized by the fact that, as American opinion polls have shown, the president's personal-popularity ratings have remained consistently high, even at times when ratings of his policies and job performance have been low.

In general, the transformation of political communication brought about by television has involved exposing the mass audience of electors to the sights and sounds of politicians speaking in a much wider range of contexts than ever before – speeches, broadcast addresses to the nation, press conferences, interviews and discussions on news and current affairs programmes, talk shows, etc. Each context imposes particular constraints on the participants, so that different ways of speaking will be seen as more or less effective in different

165

settings. Techniques which work well enough when used in addressing a political meeting or rally may therefore not come over very well on television, and those which are effective in the context of a studio discussion or interview may be quite ineffective when it comes to directly addressing a large live audience. This raises the question of how the techniques and practices that make for impressive television performances differ from those associated with impressive live oratory.

Conversation, oratory and televisuality

Just before the 1983 general election, the problems associated with coming over well on television were highlighted by a columnist in the *Observer* newspaper. In an article recommending that the then leader of the opposition should polish up his television image, Simon Hoggart noted that 'the camera prefers someone who has a more conversational tone, who doesn't address Robin Day as if he were a public meeting.' The article had begun in an even more critical vein:

'There are three things wrong with Michael Foot's appearances on television,' one of his colleagues who knows something about TV said last week. 'First, he ought to get rid of those oxy-acetylene welder's glasses. Then he should stop fidgeting. At the moment he squirms and looks around in every direction, like a timid lizard who's just shambled out into the sun. Then he should stop rambling on all the time.'
(Simon Hoggart, *Observer*, 24 April 1983)

The author's main theme was that Mr Foot had cut his political teeth at a time when oratory was still the all important factor in politics, and had subsequently failed to adapt himself to the new demands of communicating with a mass audience of television viewers. As can be seen from the above extract, the article also showed how observations of apparently minor details can be combined together to form the basis of a highly generalized and damaging assessment of a politician's image.

The fact that small details in a speaker's verbal and non-verbal behaviour may appear very noticeable and exaggerated when seen in close-up on the small screen draws attention to the risks associated with anything other than a 'low-key' television performing style. Commentaries on Ronald Reagan's communicative abilities thus invariably highlight his relaxed manner. Early in 1984, for example, an article in *The Times* (26 January 1984) referred to his 'use of manipulative Hollywood techniques – the self-deprecating joke, the heart-warming anecdote, the boyish grin, the look of principled determination – even, on occasion, the catch in the voice or the hint of a tear in the eye'. A similar theme was developed four years earlier in *Time* magazine's report on his acceptance speech at the 1980 Republican convention:

> The pleasant man might have been talking across the garden fence or maybe chatting in the kitchen with the kids. He seemed relaxed and natural, but he was addressing millions of viewers and making the most important – and very likely the best – speech of his career. (*Time*, 28 July 1980)

The same point was again made six months later by veteran United States correspondent Alistair Cooke in a *Letter from America* on BBC Radio 4. He described the president's speech on taking office as the first 'conversational inaugural' in American history. It was, he said, the shortest inaugural he had ever heard, and went on to suggest that Mr Reagan's skill lay in never forgetting for a moment that the audience which matters most is not the one immediately in front of him, but the more distant millions of television viewers.

Such a view is consistent with observations of video recordings of his speeches, which reveal a marked absence of the sorts of intonational, gestural and rhythmic shifts that are so regularly used in applause-elicitation sequences. The tapes also show that delays before the applause starts are not uncommon during speeches by President Reagan, which probably results directly from the fact that he deploys too few devices for his audiences to be able to recognize that, and exactly when, they should show their approval. A low-key style of public speaking may thus involve sacrificing the local advantages associated with eliciting early or instant applause in the interests of impressing the much larger television audience.

The importance of adapting public behaviour to a style more acceptable to the informal contexts in which most television is viewed was vividly illustrated by the brief reign of Pope John

6.1 Ronald Reagan delivers what BBC correspondent Alistair Cooke described as the 'first conversational inaugural' in American history.

Paul I. Although he died only a month after his election, he was hailed in the obituaries as having been the second greatest pope of the century. His success was said to be due to the unprecedented degree of informality he brought to the papacy (which has been emulated by his successor) – he refused to have a coronation, was seen to smile a great deal and preferred walkabouts to being carried around St Peter's Square on the traditional portable throne. For television viewers around the world, the sight of a Pope being ceremonially paraded in front of the crowds by downtrodden-looking throne-bearers was thus replaced by that of a smiling human being shaking hands and chatting freely with his fellow men and women. However, while this was establishing a new and favourable image with the obituary writers and millions of others, it was having disastrous consequences for the thousands of visitors to Rome who had failed to position themselves in the front few rows of spectators. As a result, the Vatican was inundated with letters from frustrated pilgrims complaining that they had been unable to see the Pope on his substituted St Peter's Square walkabouts. By the end of the month before he died, John Paul I had already responded by reinstating the practice of being carried aloft on the portable throne. Soon after the election of his successor, the dilemma was satisfactorily resolved by the invention of the

6.2 President Reagan's informal style even extends to encounters with royalty as in this airport meeting with the Duke of Edinburgh.

'Popemobile'. This has had the effect of making such scenes appear less formal and ostentatious in the eyes of television audiences, while at the same time maximizing papal visibility for the benefit of those who go to the trouble and expense of seeing John Paul II in person.

If less formal behavioural and conversational styles of speaking create favourable impressions with television viewers, it is presumably because they are more closely aligned with the way people behave in the comfort of their own homes – where they relax, speak conversationally to each other and sit a 'conversational distance' away from their television screens. The performers who behave and speak in similarly relaxed ways are the ones most likely to become the superstars of the small screen. The success of entertainers like Perry Como, George Burns, Val Doonican and Dave Allen has thus been widely attributed to their ability to produce relaxed performances on camera. And, in the world of politics, much the same can be said of Franklin Roosevelt's 'fireside chats' and the more recent screen appeal of Ronald Reagan.

While television viewers may find an informal conversational style particularly acceptable in their living-rooms, it does not necessarily follow that they also prefer being spoken *to* in this way from the small screen. Indeed, it is not at all clear that

6.3 Within three weeks of becoming Pope in 1978, John Paul I reluctantly agreed to use the gestatorial chair for the first time (above) after pilgrims complained they had been unable to see him during walkabouts. However, the invention of the 'Popemobile' has enabled John Paul II to combine papal visibility with a less formal TV image.

people are very impressed at all when addressed directly by those appearing on television. In spite of jokes and children's temporary beliefs about there being someone actually inside the box in the corner, everyone knows perfectly well that watching television does *not* involve a two-way form of communication, and that television screens are more like enlarged key-holes which allow people to look in on personalities they would otherwise seldom if ever see (such as popes and politicians). Indeed, there is a great deal of evidence to suggest that the secret of successful television lies in the presentation of events in such a way that viewers can feel they are *eavesdropping* on a scene, rather than being spoken to directly from the screen.

The idea that television viewers have a preference for eavesdropping is supported by the fact that only a tiny proportion of televised output actually features a speaker directly addressing the people at home. The obvious exceptions are found in news bulletins, weather forecasts, continuity announcements and the occasional address to the nation by a politician. Even in news programmes, however, the proportion of time actually given over to newsreaders speaking straight to the camera is fairly small compared with that devoted to showing viewers pictures of the day's newsworthy people and events. And interviewees, it may be noted, are routinely briefed to look at the interviewer and to treat the experience as an 'ordinary conversation'. What appears on screen are pictures of one person talking to another rather than directly to the viewers. Similarly, the most popular variety programmes, quizzes and talk shows tend to involve a live studio audience, which again means that the television audience has the experience of looking in on a live performance. Meanwhile, the ratings are regularly dominated by soap operas, serials, plays and films, all of which give viewers an extended opportunity to eavesdrop on other people's lives.

For politicians who have been accustomed to communicating directly with live audiences, this wider range of circumstances in which they may be exposed to a mass public presents them with a set of new challenges. In addition to making speeches, they now have to be prepared to be seen being interviewed, going on walkabouts, canvassing voters, chatting to factory workers, kissing babies, stroking dogs, climbing in and out of cars and aeroplanes, greeting foreign statesmen, eating, drinking, shooting, fishing, jogging, and almost any other activity to which camera crews can get access. Not only do the masses see much more of what they are doing and how they conduct themselves, but they are also able to draw their own conclusions from what they see about the *kind of person* a particular politician is – and to do so without having to rely so exclusively on the published texts of speeches, or the second-hand reports and interpretations of journalists. Indeed professional impressionists like Mike Yarwood can make a good living from an art which depends entirely on the assumption that audiences are sufficiently familiar with small details in the appearance, sound and mannerisms of celebrities to be able to recognize and appreciate impersonations of them.

Some politicians have been quicker and more perceptive than others in seeing how the potential of television can be most effectively exploited. The late Robert McKenzie, political scientist and television commentator, considered that Harold Macmillan was the first leading British politician fully to appreciate and come to terms with the new demands of television. Towards the end of the 1950s McKenzie was telephoned by Macmillan shortly before they were scheduled to do an interview for BBC Television. It is reported that Macmillan was concerned that, because McKenzie was a neutral by-stander, it would be impossible to have a proper argument with him. He therefore proposed that they should get a known opponent of his policies to take part in the programme, and suggested Hugh Cudlipp of the *Daily Mirror*. According to McKenzie, this suggestion was regarded at the time as completely innovative, but it was eventually decided to risk the experiment. He also reported that 'Macmillan's eyes lit up the moment he saw Cudlipp', and that the liveliness of the argument which followed was deemed to be such 'good television' that it prompted a major change in BBC policy on the staging of political interviews. It also took place at around the same time as the young Robin Day had abandoned his ambition to become a barrister in favour of devoting his adversarial talents to the development of a new style of interviewing on the then recently created commercial television network. By the early 1960s, the era when deferential television interviewers would politely

6.4 Harold Macmillan and Harold Wilson are often considered to have been the first British prime ministers who fully appreciated the importance of television for politicians.

invite politicians to address the viewers directly and say whatever they liked about anything they chose was at an end.

Harold Wilson then became the first British prime minister to cultivate a low-key style in his public appearances. By puffing his pipe in public, drinking pints of beer in working-men's clubs, eating HP sauce, wearing a Gannex macintosh and taking holidays in a modest bungalow, he came across as a thoroughly ordinary chap with little taste for the more ostentatious trappings of power. He was also the first politician to discover how an utterly simple conversational device could be used to neutralize, albeit temporarily, the forceful interviewing style of Robin Day. By calling him 'Robin' in front of the viewers, he established an air of familiarity between them that made it look as though here were two quite good friends, merely going through the motions of a searching interrogation. More recently, Mrs Thatcher's advisers during the 1979 general election made the most of situations which have become increasingly accessible to television cameras as outside broadcasting technology has improved. Fearing that her performances in interviews and speeches might create an unfavourable public image of her, they encouraged her to spend a greater proportion of her time on visits and walkabouts. As a result, television viewers saw much more of her 'chatting naturally' with ordinary people up and down the country than would otherwise have been the case.

However, the number of politicians who have so far succeeded, like Ronald Reagan, in bringing a low-key conversational style to the live public speech are very few and far between. Martin Luther King had in fact gone some way in this direction by omitting expansive non-verbal actions from his oratory, and by standing almost motionless while delivering his speeches. John F. Kennedy's televisual appeal during the broadcast debate with Richard Nixon prior to the 1960 presidential election was also hailed as a critical factor in his victory. A majority of those who heard the speeches on radio considered that Nixon had won, whereas the majority of those who saw them on television considered Kennedy the winner. Radio listeners heard only the accomplished lawyer arguing his case, and never saw the dark shadow on Nixon's apparently unshaven face, nor the beads of sweat glistening under the television lights – details which were widely regarded as crucial to Nixon's downfall. More recently, television news pictures of François Mitterrand leaning casually on a lectern and apparently 'chatting' to some very large audiences contrasted sharply with the more traditional style of public speaking employed by his competitors in the 1981 French presidential election.

For those skilled in the traditional techniques of spellbinding oratory, the advent of mass television coverage is a very mixed

6.5   The 1960 Kennedy-Nixon debate: radio listeners and television viewers came to different conclusions as to who had won.

blessing. They may stand a better chance of having excerpts from their speeches replayed on television news programmes, but their overall image may actually suffer from such exposure. The reasons for this are similar to the reasons why stage productions of live plays and operas do not make good television. Adapting classical works for television is a notoriously difficult thing to do well, but television companies invariably go to the trouble of producing their own versions in preference to the apparently easier option of sending camera crews into West End theatres. Similarly, the broadcasting media have only made limited use of the hundreds of hours of recorded parliamentary proceedings that are available to them, and the few samples that are played over the air have done little to improve the public image of politicians.

The central problem would seem to be that the performing techniques which work effectively in theatres, opera houses and parliaments are used with a large live audience in mind, and were never designed to be overheard by groups of two or three people sitting in their own homes. Practices which are visible, audible and impressive to those sitting in the back row of an auditorium or debating chamber are therefore likely to seem grossly exaggerated, unnatural and even oppressive when viewed on a small screen from a distance of a few feet. A booming voice, poetic phrases, finely co-ordinated intonational cadences and expansive non-verbal actions are unlikely to impress when witnessed at close quarters. As far as the last of these is concerned, it is noticeable that television hardly ever features personalities who gesticulate extensively while talking. And the few who have managed to get away with it have to be prepared, like the popularizers of science Magnus Pyke and David Bellamy, to be regarded as eccentrics.

If traditional oratory is likely to be seen as over-done or over-acted when viewed through the zoom lens, those with a talent for it may have difficulty in adapting their communicative style for the purposes of lower-key studio interviews and discussions. In answering questions, they may have trouble expressing themselves with an appropriate degree of succinctness. Being keyed-up is probably essential when delivering a spellbinding speech, but it is a positive disadvantage in an interview, where it will merely make the speaker appear unduly intense, nervous and even shifty. Orators are also used to being able to make the same speech night after night to different audiences, but to be seen saying the same thing in different interviews not only sounds rehearsed and lacking in spontaneity, but will eventually bore and irritate viewers. Television places a high priority on novelty and variety, and audiences are quick to react against repetition.

Now that we have entered an era in which oratory is only one of a number of different ways in which politicians get to be seen and heard by a wider public, those who have mastered its techniques therefore face two major problems. One is that the televising of a spellbinding performance can make a speaker look like a fanatical demagogue to viewers. And the other is that to rely on techniques of oratory in a studio interview or discussion is to run the risk of coming across as long-winded, tense and generally lacking in spontaneity.

A major consequence of all this, which is symbolized by the spectacular success of Ronald Reagan, is that the basis on which the popular appeal of politicians is established is undergoing a

6.6
Michael Foot
(above) and
Roy Jenkins
(below) who
led Labour and
the SDP into the
1983 campaign.
Both attracted
criticism for
their lack of
televisual
appeal, and
have since been
replaced as
party leaders.

major transformation. In the past, mastery of the traditional techniques of oratory was essential for anyone hoping to get to the top in politics. But we can expect more and more of our future political leaders to be drawn from among those who have achieved mastery of the more relaxed conversational style that comes across more effectively on television.

However, it is unlikely that things will go quite so far in Britain as they have done in the United States, where presidents are not required to perform daily in congressional debates and can therefore rely more heavily, and regularly, on screen-performing ability. So long as British prime ministers have to be able to survive the rough and tumble of Commons debates, and especially Prime Minister's Question Time, it is unlikely that the job will ever be held by anyone who cannot hold his own as a reasonably accomplished orator. What is more likely is that political parties will increasingly select all-rounders to be their leaders – people who are capable of creating a good impression both as orators *and* as television performers.

Of the main British political parties, only the Conservatives under Margaret Thatcher and the Liberals under David Steel had equipped themselves with such all-round performers as leaders by the time of the 1983 election. Labour's Michael Foot and the Social Democrats' Roy Jenkins both came under fire during the campaign for their lack of televisual appeal. Since then, however, they have been replaced by Neil Kinnock and David Owen respectively. Not only are the new leaders twenty years younger than their predecessors, but they are also generally recognized as effective performers both on television and in parliament. The fact that Kinnock has been nicknamed the 'Welsh Windbag' suggests that there is room for improvement in his live oratory, but there are few who dispute his televisual appeal. David Owen, on the other hand, is rated highly as a parliamentary debater, but has attracted a certain amount of adverse comment for being rather too earnest and lacking in humour when appearing on television. None the less, both would seem to qualify as competent all-rounders, and their election as leaders means that the main British political parties have now all opted for a style of leadership best suited to modern conditions.

It remains to be seen, of course, if the changes now taking place in the types of people who become our political masters will make much difference in the long run to the quality of government. Whether 'conversational' presidents and prime ministers turn out to be any better or worse than orators at managing the affairs of state is a question which will have to be left to future generations of historians.

Understanding televisuality

A central concern of this book has been to show that detailed observation of the interaction between public speakers and their audiences makes it possible to identify and describe basic components in the machinery through which effective oratory is produced. However, the dynamics of mass television appeal are much further from being properly understood, and are more resistant to exposure by the application of similar analytic methods. This is partly because of the problem of getting comparable access to the particular passages in broadcasts which evoke an immediate and favourable response from television audiences. Given that they do not applaud, it will be more difficult to find equivalent responses to use as evidence of their approval. It is also more difficult to wire up enough living-rooms with all the equipment necessary for recording such observations, than it is to collect tapes of public speeches.

Other problems arise from the more complicated nature of the interaction that takes place in televised interviews and discussions. As was noted earlier, the high degree of standardization and the simplicity of the techniques used by orators result from the constraints associated with holding the attention and interest of large crowds. By contrast, there is much greater scope for variation in the behaviour of participants in the more conversational programmes watched by television audiences. The fact that viewers are isolated from the vast majority of others who are tuned into any particular programme also makes a critical difference, as it prevents anyone's immediate reaction to what a politician says from being influenced by the way large numbers of others around them are responding (as when a burst of applause gets under way). Individual television viewers are thus much freer to draw their own conclusions from what they see and hear than are audiences at public meetings.

This independence of the individuals in the mass television audience, coupled with the greater flexibility and subtlety of televised discussions, also creates more scope for a wider variety of personal opinions about what features of a performance are most relevant for making assessments. Different people will have different priorities about what are the most desirable characteristics for a politician to exhibit, and there is a considerable range of possibilities: commitment, niceness, toughness, decisiveness, honesty, clarity, humour, idealism, physical appearance, mannerisms, clothes, hairstyles, and so on. If these and other factors are relevant to the way audiences interpret the behaviour and personalities of politicians, a fuller understanding of the processes involved in their assessment

6.7 Three youthful and televisual challengers to Margaret Thatcher in 1988? From left: Neil Kinnock (Labour); David Steel (Liberal); David Owen (Social Democratic Party).

will depend on answers being found to a much more general question, namely how do people go about interpreting each other's behaviour in any kind of conversational setting? For we are all engaged in a more or less continual process of analysing and interpreting the verbal and non-verbal conduct of other people, and thereby coming to far-reaching conclusions about what kind of people they are. In the main, our likes and dislikes derive directly from detailed observations of how a person speaks and responds in the course of everyday conversational encounters, observations which we are often hardly aware of making at the time, and which are hardly ever explicitly articulated with any degree of precision.

If we are to learn more about how politicians create a favourable impression on television audiences, it will therefore be necessary first to know a good deal more than is currently known about how people in general create favourable impressions in the course of similarly informal exchanges. Although there is a good deal of contemporary concern about the manipulative techniques deployed by politicians, advertising agencies and public-relations consultants, there is no reason to believe either that they have fully grasped this point or that they are in possession of secret knowledge about the workings of conversational communication. For the fact is that, until very recently, everyday conversation was regarded as far too ordinary and insignificant to merit detailed observational analysis by social and behavioural scientists, or by anyone else. The findings reported in this book, however, were only made possible by adopting exactly the opposite view, and they suggest that the workings of conversation may be far too important a matter to be ignored for much longer.

Appendix I
Career summaries
of the politicians cited

The following is a complete list of all the politicians quoted or referred to in the main part of the book, together with brief career details. They are listed by the forms of name by which they are best known, and titles (Sir, Lord, Lady, Right Honourable, etc.) have been omitted.

Andropov, Yuri, 1914–84. General secretary of the Communist Party of the USSR and president of the presidium of the Supreme Soviet (1982–4).

Attlee, Clement, 1883–1967. Labour prime minister (1945–51); deputy prime minister in Churchill's wartime cabinet (1942–5); leader of the Opposition (1951–5); Labour MP for Limehouse (1922–50) and West Walthamstow (1950–5).

Bandaranaike, Sirimavo, born 1916. Prime minister of Sri Lanka (1960–5 and 1970–7).

Benn, Anthony Wedgwood, born 1925. Labour MP for Bristol South East (1950–60 and 1963–83) and Chesterfield since 1984; postmaster-general (1964–6); minister of technology (1966–70), industry (1974–5) and energy (1975–9).

Bevan, Aneurin, 1897–1960. Labour MP for Ebbw Vale (1929–60); minister of health (1945–51) and of labour and national service (1951).

Boyle, Edward, 1923–82. Conservative MP for Birmingham Handsworth (1950–70); minister of education and science (1962–4); vice-chancellor of Leeds University (1970–82).

Brezhnev, Leonid, 1906–82. General secretary of the Communist Party of the USSR (1964–82) and president of the presidium of the Supreme Soviet (1977–82).

Callaghan, James, born 1912. Labour prime minister (1976–9); leader of the Opposition (1979–80); MP for Cardiff South (1945–50) and Cardiff South East (since 1950); chancellor of the exchequer (1964–7); home secretary (1967–70); foreign secretary (1974–6).

Castro, Fidel, born 1927. Communist prime minister of Cuba (1959–76); head of state and president of the Council of State since 1976.

Chernenko, Konstantin, 1912–85. General secretary of the Communist Party of the USSR and president of the Supreme Soviet 1984–5.

Churchill, Winston, 1874–1965. Conservative prime minister (1940–5 and 1951–5); leader of the Opposition (1945–51); MP for Epping (1924–45) and Woodford (1945–64), having formerly sat also as a Liberal MP.

Crosland, Anthony, 1918–77. Labour MP for Grimsby (1959–77); minister for economic affairs (1964–5) and of education and science (1965–7); president of the Board of Trade (1967–9); minister for local government (1969–70) and the environment (1974–6).

de Gaulle, Charles, 1890–1970. French general and first president of the Fifth Republic (1958–69); leader of the Free French from London during the Second World War; temporarily headed the provisional government in 1944.

Foot, Michael, born 1913. Labour MP for Ebbw Vale since 1960; party leader and leader of the Opposition (1980–3); minister of employment (1974–6); leader of the House of Commons (1976–9).

Gaitskell, Hugh, 1906–63. Labour MP for Leeds South (1945–63); party leader and leader of the Opposition (1955–63); minister of fuel and power (1946–7); chancellor of the exchequer (1950–1).

Gandhi, Indira, 1917–84. Prime minister of India (1966–77 and 1980–4); president of the Indian National Congress 1978–84.

Healey, Denis, born 1917. Labour MP for Leeds South East (1952–5) and Leeds East since 1955; minister of defence (1964–70); chancellor of the exchequer (1974–9); deputy leader of the Labour Party (1980–3).

Heath, Edward, born 1916. Conservative prime minister (1970–4); leader of the Opposition (1965–70 and 1974–5); MP for Bexley since 1950.

Heffer, Eric, born 1922. Labour MP for Liverpool Walton since 1964.

Heseltine, Michael, born 1933. Conservative MP for Henley since 1974 and Tavistock (1966–74); minister for the environment (1979–82) and defence (since 1982).

Hitler, Adolf, 1889–1945. Nazi chancellor of Germany (1933–45).

Howe, Geoffrey, born 1926. Conservative MP for Surrey East since 1974 and Reigate (1970–4); foreign secretary since 1983; chancellor of the exchequer (1979–83).

Jackson, Jesse, born 1941. Black American minister and civil rights campaigner. Candidate for the Democratic presidential nomination, 1984.

Jeger, Lena, born 1915. Labour MP for Holborn and St Pancras South (1953–9 and 1974–9); Labour Party National Executive Committee (1968–80).

Jenkins, Roy, born 1920. Social Democratic MP for Glasgow Hillhead since 1982. Labour MP for Southwark Central (1948–50) and Birmingham Stetchford (1950–76); home secretary (1965–7); chancellor of the exchequer (1967–70); deputy leader of the Labour Party (1970–2); president of the European Commission (1977–81); co-founder of the Social Democratic Party in 1981 and leader until 1983.

Johnson, Lyndon B., 1908–73. Thirty-sixth president of the

United States (Democrat) (1963–8); vice-president (1961–3).

Kennedy, John F., 1917–63. Thirty-fifth president of the United States (Democrat) (1961–3).

Khomeini, Ayatollah, born 1902. Leader of the Islamic Revolution and ruler of Iran since 1979.

King, Martin Luther, 1929–68. Black American minister and leader of the civil rights movement.

Kinnock, Neil, born 1942. Labour Party leader and leader of the Opposition since 1983; MP for Bedwelty since 1970.

Lenin, Vladimir Ilych, 1870–1924. Bolshevik leader of the Russian Revolution and first head of government of the USSR.

Lincoln, Abraham, 1809–65. Sixteenth president of the United States (Republican) (1861–5).

Macleod, Iain, 1913–70. Conservative MP for Enfield West (1950–70); minister of health (1952–5), labour (1955–9) and the colonies (1959–61); leader of the House of Commons (1961–4); chancellor of the exchequer (June–July 1970).

Macmillan, Harold, born 1894. Conservative prime minister (1957–63); MP for Stockton-on-Tees (1924–9 and 1931–45) and Bromley (1945–64); minister of housing (1951–4) and defence (1954–5); foreign secretary (April–December 1955); chancellor of the exchequer (1955–7).

Meir, Golda, 1898–1978. Labour prime minister of Israel (1969–74).

Mitterrand, François, born 1916. Socialist president of France since 1981.

Murray, Len, born 1922. General secretary of the Trades Union Congress since 1973.

Mussolini, Benito, 1883–1945. Italian Fascist dictator (1922–45).

Nixon, Richard M., born 1913. Thirty-seventh president of the United States (Republican) (1969–74); vice-president (1953–61).

Owen, David, born 1938. Leader of the Social Democratic Party since 1983; MP for Plymouth Devenport since 1974 (Labour 1974–81; SDP since 1981) and Labour MP for Plymouth Sutton (1966–74); minister of health (1974–6); foreign secretary (1977–9).

Pardoe, John, born 1934. Former Liberal MP for North Cornwall (1966–79).

Parkinson, Cecil, born 1931. Conservative MP for Hertfordshire South (since 1974) and Enfield West (1970–4). Chancellor of the Duchy of Lancaster (1982–3); minister for trade and industry (June–September 1983); chairman of the Conservative Party (1981–3).

Perón, Isabelita, born 1930. President of Argentina (1974–6); vice-president (1973–4).

Powell, Enoch, born 1912. Ulster Unionist MP for South Down since 1974 and Conservative MP for Wolverhampton South West (1950–74). Minister of health (1960–3).

Prior, James, born 1927. Conservative MP for Lowestoft since 1959; minister for Northern Ireland since 1981; minister of agriculture (1970–2); leader of the House of Commons (1972–4); minister for employment (1979–81).

Ray, Robert, born 1928. Republican governor of Iowa since 1968.

Reagan, Ronald, born 1911. Fortieth president of the United States (Republican) since 1981; governor of California (1967–74).

Roosevelt, Franklin D., 1884–1945. Thirty-second president of the United States (Democrat) (1932–45).

Shore, Peter, born 1924. Labour MP for Stepney since 1964; minister for economic affairs (1967–9), trade (1974–6) and the environment (1976–9).

Stalin, Joseph, 1879–1953. General secretary to the Central Committee of the Communist Party of the USSR (1922–53).

Steel, David, born 1938. Leader of the Liberal Party since 1976; MP for Roxburgh, Selkirk and Peebles since 1965.

St John-Stevas, Norman, born 1929. Conservative MP for Chelmsford since 1964; leader of the House of Commons and minister for the arts (1979–81).

Tebbit, Norman, born 1931. Conservative MP for Chingford since 1974 and Epping (1970–74); minister for trade and industry since 1983; minister for employment (1981–3).

Thatcher, Margaret, born 1925. Conservative prime minister since 1979; MP for Finchley since 1959; minister of education and science (1970–4); leader of the Opposition (1975–9).

Wallace, George, born 1919. Governor of Alabama (1963–7) and since 1971.

Whitelaw, William, born 1918. Deputy leader of the Conservative Party since 1975; MP for Penrith (1955–83); leader of the House of Commons (1970–2); minister for Northern Ireland (1972–3) and employment (1973–4); home secretary (1979–83).

Wilson, Harold, born 1916. Labour prime minister (1964–70 and 1974–6); MP for Huyton (1945–83); leader of the Opposition (1963–4 and 1970–4); president of the Board of Trade (1947–50).

Wilson, Woodrow, 1856–1924. Twenty-eighth president of the United States (Democrat) (1912–20).

Appendix II
Transcription symbols, methods and exercises

Glossary of transcription symbols

Example	*Explanation*
Audience: XXXXXXXXX	Loud applause
Audience: xxxxxxxxx	Quiet applause
Audience: –x–	Isolated/single clap
Audience: –x–x–xx–	Spasmodic/hesitant clapping
Audience: xxxXXXXXxxx	Applause amplitude increases/decreases
⊢——(8.0)——⊣ Audience: –x–xxXXXXxxx–	Duration of applause from onset (or completion of overlapping talk) to nearest tenth of a second. *NB*: number of X's (or x's) does *not* indicate duration of applause, except where it overlaps with talk (see next example)
Speaker: ... for ⌐Alien └x-XXXXXX	Onset of applause with continuation through and beyond overlapping talk
S: ⌐ it is wrong (0.5) to-uhh A:└XXXXXXXXXXXXXXXXXX	Applause continues while an overlapping speaker pauses for half a second before continuing to talk in overlap

189

↑ Shadow minist ↓ er	Upward/downward intonation in immediately following particle
(0.5) (.)	Numbers indicate pause lengths to nearest tenth of a second. Dot indicates micropause (less than 0.2 seconds)
hhh	In-breath or out-breath – the more h's the longer the duration
I <u>say</u> to y ↑ <u>OU</u>	Capital letters indicate more loudly spoken particles. Underlining indicates extra emphasis

Methods

The transcriptions in this book have all been simplified from more detailed originals. The symbols listed above are, apart from those representing applause, a small proportion of the continually expanding set which has been developed by Gail Jefferson and is now widely used by conversation analysts. A fuller glossary and more extended discussion of this method of transcription can be found in J. M. Atkinson and J. C. Heritage (eds) (1984) *Structures of Social Action: Studies in Conversation Analysis* (Cambridge and New York, Cambridge University Press).

Readers interested in pursuing work of this sort for themselves should note that transcribing is not necessary merely to produce written reports on analyses of audio and video tape-recordings. It is also an essential part of the observational process, requiring the constant use of replay facilities and vigilant attention to detail. It is thus not unusual to spend an hour in producing a satisfactorily accurate transcript of one minute's worth of talk. However, although it is very time-consuming and calls for intense concentration, anyone seriously interested in making discoveries should resist the temptation to delegate the task to an audio-typist or research assistant. This is because it is usually in the course of listening to tapes closely enough to transcribe them that one begins, on a good day, to notice recurring details in the talk, and to ask what they are doing there, how they are being responded to, and how they compare with the workings of other similar or different interactional sequences.

A key part of this observational process is to have as few preconceptions as possible about what is likely to be interesting or uninteresting: the challenge is to bend over backwards to regard the data as, in Harold Garfinkel's words, 'anthropologically strange'. In other words, one of the most difficult things to do in studying the workings of talk is to adopt a stance of puzzlement and curiosity about something that is so utterly familiar. However, once we can admit that we do not necessarily know how to describe activities that we do easily (like talking or riding a bicycle), we can begin to find mystery in how we do even the most ordinary things.

The experience of conversation analysts to date suggests that it always pays to transcribe in as much detail as possible, even though the resulting hieroglyphics may eventually have to be simplified in the interests of readability. This is because interpersonal communication is itself conducted at extraordinary, yet to be ascertained levels of detail. It also involves a range of audible and visible elements (including words, intonation, pronunciation, stress, pace and rhythm, gaze, head movements, postural shifts, gesticulations and spatial positioning). It is clear that these can be deployed together in a variety of more or less subtle ways, though there is still a very long way to go towards clarifying exactly how such processes work. If progress is to be made in this direction, it is essential to pay attention to whatever details manifest themselves in communicative behaviour, and not to assume that one or other dimension can ever be safely ignored.

When it comes to learning how to carry out such observational studies, there is no substitute for extensive practice with the raw materials. It is also useful to watch or listen to tapes in the company of others, with whom one can compare notes about what appears to be going on in some particular sequence. One way of getting started is for each member of a group or class to transcribe the same excerpt from a tape and then to agree on a version of the transcript. This can result in lengthy and lively discussions about details of the talk and how best to represent them in written form, and it will often be necessary to defer more analytic deliberations until a later meeting.

With an agreed transcript and tape-recorder to hand, it is possible to get a data-analysis workshop under way. One procedure that works reasonably well is to begin by listening several times to the equivalent of two or three pages of transcript, as a prelude to selecting a shorter segment for closer scrutiny. As to how such selections should be made, there are no firm rules. However, if the principle 'go for anything that sounds interesting for whatever reason' is followed, it is surprising how often the same segment is chosen by several of those present. Once it has been agreed on, this shorter excerpt should be replayed a few times. When everyone has heard or seen enough of the tape, it is worth spending ten or fifteen minutes in silence, while each person writes notes on features of the data that struck them as interesting. The participants can then take it in turns to summarize their notes before embarking on a more open discussion. Again, the best rule to follow as to what to jot down is to 'write about anything that seems interesting', a policy which also sometimes results in a close consensus on certain points.

Although such workshops are useful for familiarizing people with the idea of doing detailed observational studies of communicative processes, it must be stressed that not too much should be expected from them as far as producing new analyses is concerned. This is partly because it will almost always be necessary to follow up hunches with reference to a much larger collection of data than can be examined in the course of an hour or two. However, such sessions can be very useful as a source of ideas about what might be worth investigating in greater detail.

It is also possible, of course, to take a less open-ended approach by, for example, studying tapes with reference to existing research findings, with a view to finding similar instances of the practices described, checking how far the earlier results hold in the face of new data, or perhaps producing a more detailed analysis. This is one of the reasons for including below a list of possible follow-up exercises or projects suggested by the findings reported in the main part of this book. Another is that a number of teachers have told me that they see considerable potential in this type of work for courses in sociology and communications studies, and have regularly asked for more guidance as to how this potential could be realized. Most schools and colleges nowadays are equipped with audio and video recording technology, though there appears to be a good deal of uncertainty about how such equipment can be most effectively used for teaching purposes. This appendix, then, is intended as a first step in responding positively to such needs.

List of exercises and follow-up projects

The findings reported in this book suggest that, in addition to exercises in transcription and data-analysis workshops of the sort listed above, the following tasks would be worth pursuing further.

1 Checking out the main results of the work reported here with reference to newly collected data from radio and television.

2 Expanding and improving the analysis by looking for other verbal and non-verbal devices involved in the applause-elicitation process.

3 Examining more closely the workings of such vocal phenomena as intonation, stress, rhythm, pace, phasing (pause positioning, etc.), pitch and volume, as well as non-vocal features such as gaze, head movements, postural shifts and use of gestures.

4 Analysing the public-speaking styles of particular individuals − e.g. what effect has Mrs Thatcher's use of the 'sincerity machine' had on her mode of delivery? How do President Reagan's scripted and unscripted performances compare?

5 Looking more closely at the factors involved in the production of boring or otherwise ineffective public speeches.

6 Identifying what prompts disaffiliative responses such as booing and heckling. What techniques do speakers use in responding to such interventions? Which ones deal with the problem most effectively?

7 Looking at the workings of debates in legislative assemblies such as the UK Parliament and the US Congress.

8 Studying the relationship between audience responses to speeches and media reportage.

9 Analysing the structure of whole speeches (e.g. President Reagan's inaugural, Neil Kinnock's acceptance of the Labour Party leadership and older classics like 'I have a dream' and 'Ich bin ein Berliner').

10 Collecting comparative data from other countries. How far do the same devices work in the same way in different cultures and languages?

11 Reading persuasive or polemical texts with a view to discovering what verbal devices writers use to package their messages and arguments.

12 Recording and analysing the workings of other multi-party settings where different forms of public speaking are involved; e.g. in church services, debates, meetings, courtrooms, classrooms and lecture theatres.

Appendix III
Selected references

Books on conversation analysis

There are as yet no standard textbooks devoted exclusively to providing a straightforward introduction to conversation analysis. However, most collections of research papers and monograph-length reports contain a certain amount of relevant introductory discussion. Among the books listed here, extended introductions and summaries are contained in Atkinson and Drew (1979), Goodwin (1981), Levinson (1983), Heritage (1984), and Atkinson and Heritage (1984). Readers interested in how this analytic tradition relates to sociology and linguistics are particularly recommended to consult the books by Heritage and Levinson respectively. Those with a special interest in the analysis of video-taped interactions will find Goodwin's book the most useful.

Atkinson, J. M. and Drew, P. (1979) *Order in Court: The Organisation of Verbal Interaction in Judicial Settings*, London, Macmillan Press; Atlantic Highlands, New Jersey: Humanities Press.

Atkinson, J. M. and Heritage, J. C. (eds) (1984) *Structures of Social Action: Studies in Conversation Analysis*, Cambridge and New York, Cambridge University Press.

Goodwin, C. (1981) *Conversational Organization: Interaction between Speakers and Hearers*, New York, Academic Press.

Heritage, J. C. (1984) *Garfinkel and Ethnomethodology*, Oxford, Basil Blackwell.

Levinson, S. C. (1983) *Pragmatics*, Cambridge and New York, Cambridge University Press.

Psathas, G. (1979) *Everyday Language: Studies in Ethnomethodology*, New York, Irvington.

Schenkein, J. N. (1977) *Studies in the Organization of Conversational Interaction*, New York, Academic Press.

Sudnow, D. (ed.) (1973) *Studies in Social Interaction*, New York, Free Press.

Books quoted in the text

Ayer, A. J. (1977) *Part of My Life*, London, Oxford University Press.

Marx, K. and Engels, F. (1848) *The Communist Manifesto*.

Orwell, G. (1945) *Animal Farm*, London, Secker & Warburg.

Orwell, G. (1949) *Nineteen Eighty-Four*, London, Secker & Warburg.

Quintillian, *Institutes of Oratory, or The Education of an Orator*, trans. J. S. Watson, London, Boehn, 1856.

Rousseau, J.-J. (1762) *The Social Contract*.

Solzhenitsyn, A. (1973) *The Gulag Archipelago*, New York, Harper & Row.

Wapshott, N. and Brock, G. (1983) *Thatcher*, London, Macdonald.

Research papers on which this book is based

Atkinson, J. M. (1982) 'Understanding formality: the categorisation and production of "formal" interaction', *British Journal of Sociology*, 33 (1), 86–117.

Atkinson, J. M. (1983) 'Two devices for generating audience approval: a comparative analysis of public discourse and texts', in Ehlich, K. and van Riemsdijk, H. (eds)

Connectedness in Sentence, Discourse and Text, Tilburg, Netherlands, Tilburg Papers in Linguistics.

Atkinson, J. M. (1984) 'Public speaking and audience responses: some techniques for inviting applause', in Atkinson, J. M. and Heritage, J. C. (eds) Structures of Social Action: Studies in Conversation Analysis, Cambridge and New York, Cambridge University Press.

Atkinson, J. M. (forthcoming) 'Refusing invited applause: preliminary observations from a case study of charismatic oratory', in van Dijk, T. A. (ed) Handbook of Discourse Analysis, London, Academic Press.

Atkinson, J. M. (forthcoming) 'The 1983 election and the demise of live oratory', in Crewe, I. and Harrop, M. (eds) Political Communications: the General Election Campaign of 1983, Cambridge, Cambridge University Press.

Index